"Great Gluten-Free Vegan Eats is a solid reflection of Allyson Kramer's style and a shining example of why her blog, Manifest Vegan, has become so popular. Allyson delights the senses with stunning visuals, flavorful ingredients, and simplistic recipes that will make you forget about eggs, dairy, and gluten altogether."

-ALISA FLEMING, author of *Go Dairy Free: The Guide and Cookbook* (godairyfree.org)

"Allyson Kramer's debut cookbook is the essential guide for deliciously creative, gluten-free, vegan eats! Filled with gorgeous photographs and mouthwatering recipes like Banana Berry Cobbler and Spinach Artichoke Dip, *Great Gluten-Free Vegan Eats* will inspire you to cook in a whole new way."

-JULIE HASSON, author of *Vegan Diner* (juliehasson.com)

"Being a gluten-free vegan just got a whole lot better, thanks to Allyson Kramer. In *Great Gluten-Free Vegan Eats*, Allyson dishes up a broad range of creative, tasty dishes. With beautiful photographs, this book will tempt eaters of all dietary persuasions."

-TAMASIN NOYES, author of *American Vegan Kitchen* (veganappetite.com)

"Whether you have no choice but to eat gluten-free foods, or if you simply wish to add more delicious meals made *sans gluten* to your diet, this stunningly illustrated book has your back. And if you're worried that a gluten-free diet means no more baked goods to keep your sweet tooth going, all you have to do is take one look at Allyson's Blueberry Cake Donuts, and breathe an audible sigh of relief. These are pure bliss made hole-y."

-CELINE STEEN, co-author of *Hearty Vegan Meals for Vegan Appetites*, and many more (havecakewilltravel.com)

"Allyson will show you how to make good-for-you gluten-free meals that are delicious, too. Going gluten-free has never been so easy and tasty!"

-CHRISTY MORGAN, author of *Blissful Bites: Vegan Meals That Nourish Mind, Body, and Planet* (theblissfulchef.com)

GREAT GLUTEN-FREE VEGAN EATS

CUT OUT THE GLUTEN AND ENJOY AN EVEN HEALTHIER VEGAN DIET WITH RECIPES FOR FABULOUS, ALLERGY-FREE FARE

ALLYSON KRAMER

© 2012 Fair Winds Press
Text © 2012 Allyson Kramer

First published in the USA in 2012 by
Fair Winds Press, a member of
Quayside Publishing Group
100 Cummings Center
Suite 406-L
Beverly, MA 01915-6101
www.fairwindspress.com

16 15 14 13   3 4 5

ISBN: 978-1-59233-513-8

Digital edition published in 2012
eISBN-13: 978-1-61058-404-3

Library of Congress Cataloging-in-Publication Data available

Book and cover design by Rita Sowins / Sowins Design
Photography by Allyson Kramer

Printed and bound in China

The information in this book is for educational purposes only. It is not intended to replace the advice of a physician or medical practitioner. Please see your health care provider before beginning any new health program.

DEDICATION

This cookbook is dedicated to my dad,
Larney Wendell Cain. As a wonderful father
should, he helped me think critically
and taught me to follow my dreams and hold
true to my values despite what anyone
had to say about them. He is my light in the
dimly lit trail of life, and his passion
and conviction for simply being a good
person will carry me through whatever
I pursue. I miss him dearly, but still
heed his guidance every single day.

CONTENTS

INTRODUCTION

Welcome to the wonderful world of gluten-free vegan eating! Some of you may have stumbled upon this book and thought to yourselves ... gluten-free *and* vegan? Why both?

In short, this book is intended for people who *cannot* or *choose not* to eat animal products or gluten. Some people arrive at this type of diet by medical necessity (like vegans who have celiac disease or multiple allergy sufferers); others just enjoy cutting down on gluten and animal products because they feel better doing so. This book is not a low-fat book, a sugar-free book, or a book claiming to save the world. My intention here is to show people how incredibly easy it is to enjoy delicious foods that are 100 percent vegan and gluten-free. I'd like it to be an introduction to this wonderful way of eating for those unfamiliar with this "double diet" and a source of inspiration for all the seasoned gluten-free vegan eaters out there. This is a cookbook for vegans, gluten-free folks, and everyone in between.

My Story

I've been a committed vegan for more than five years now, and consider myself hooked for life. (If you are interested in learning more about veganism, please have a look at the Vegan Resources page [page 214] provided in the back of this book. This guide is full of information explaining these reasons more thoroughly and eloquently than I could ever attempt to do in this introduction.)

Vegans have a variety of reasons for choosing not to eat animal-based foods and by-products, ranging from ethical to strictly dietary. We are not a unified group of people, nor are we consistent in our message a lot of times. For me, veganism is a crucial part of trying my hardest to lead a nonviolent life. But, there are countless other great reasons that I am proud to be a vegan, from helping to decrease my carbon footprint to having the opportunity to enjoy an enormous amount of veggies and other plant-based foods as the centerpiece of my daily meals.

A few years back, I was diagnosed with celiac disease after suffering from years of chronic pain and other symptoms that left me scratching my head as to what was wrong with me. Turns out, gluten was the issue. So I had to quit cold Tofurky. And once I cut out gluten, I regained my health completely.

I know what some of you are thinking.

But what's left to eat?

Plenty.

In fact, *tons*! It may sound hard to believe, but stay with me here. Growing up, I was your standard non-picky omnivore with a preference for potatoes, cheese, and animal-product-laden baked goods. Crusty white bread was what I based most of my meals around, and vegetables rarely made an appearance anywhere but as a side dish on my dinner plate. The foods I loved most contained plenty of meat, butter, eggs, and cheese. Decadent, yes, but that was tradition, and those were the foods I knew and loved.

The honest truth is that even though I am vegan by choice, and gluten-free by necessity, I still crave the traditional foods I grew up with. Yes, even the animal-product-laden ones. Does this mean I'm pining for a deep-fried leg of a chicken? No. What I crave are the flavors and textures that remind me of my childhood. Just because I no longer choose to support the killing and abuse of animals—and my body rejects gluten—doesn't mean I have to give up eating seriously good food.

Going vegan was an easy transition for me, mostly due to the fact that I made the *choice* to be vegan. But, when it came to giving up gluten, I felt like my world came crashing down—at least temporarily. I had the same problem trying to wrap my head around going gluten-free as many people do when faced with going vegan. What the heck was I supposed to eat? Baking was my first love, and without wheat I felt helpless, hopeless, and not at all in my element. After perusing most of the gluten-free cookbooks available, I was left with one "solution": eggs. Most gluten-free baked good recipes I've come across contain upwards of ten eggs per recipe! Yuck, and no thank you.

So what was a girl to do? Simple: I cried, I whined, and I made about forty-five batches of inedible sludge. It was torture.

Then it clicked.

Since I already understood how to use plant-based substitutes for equally delicious re-sults, shouldn't it be easy to replace wheat with non-glutinous grains?

Turns out, it was. And I can show you how, too. With a little know-how, you'll see that gluten-free vegan eating is simple … and dare I say *fun*?

There's really no need to give up your favorite comfort foods when eating vegan and gluten-free. In fact, I'd like to show you all the wonderful foods you *can* eat! This book is a collection of some of my most cherished recipes—I hope you find a few that become your favorites, too!

Final Recipe Note

When you hit the recipes section, use it as a template. Once you've made the dish and un-derstand the final product and what all the components add up to, change it up to suit your tastes. Make the recipes personal. Make them yours.

THE GLUTEN-FREE VEGAN PANTRY & BASICS

Making great gluten-free vegan
eats is simple once you have
some basics ironed out.
Use this guide to help you
understand the ingredients found
in this book and inspire you to
make some of your own delicious
gluten-free vegan creations.

GLUTEN-FREE FLOUR GUIDE

The most important thing to understand when cooking and baking without gluten is that there isn't one "all-purpose" flour. Instead, many flours are used in combination to achieve varying results.

Prepackaged gluten-free baking mixes are available, but they're usually just a simple combination of flours and starches along with a little xanthan gum added for binding power. I find it more enjoyable to make up individual flour blends for whatever I happen to be making. This way, I can better control the texture, add a little nutritional boost wherever it's needed, and tailor the results based on the specific flours used. Although it may seem pricey at first to have to stock up on many different flours just to make cookies one day and a cake the next, it often ends up being a little easier on your wallet in the long run than buying proprietary mixes. Also, there is always the option of grinding your own flours, which is as simple as purchasing a grain mill (available in a range of prices) and some whole grains to grind. Most people with the capability of doing so prefer grinding their own over purchasing preground flours because the end result is a fresher, better tasting flour, but since I don't own a grain mill, I usually just purchase my flours and store them in airtight containers to keep them fresh.

The flours I have included in this list are the ones I keep stocked in my own pantry. The more you experiment with different gluten-free flours, the better you will understand their unique properties and where they work best in cooking and baking. I like to vary my own flour blends with each new recipe I create, so I don't have a basic blend I use or recommend, but I highly encourage you to experiment with the different flours to see what you like best. As with anything, practice makes perfect!

Almond Meal

A great source of protein and calcium, this flour is made from ground blanched almonds and is pale yellow in color. It adds a warm flavor and a good dose of moisture to baked goods when used alone or in combination with other flours or starches.

Brown Rice Flour

Brown rice flour is simply ground whole-grain brown rice and is full of nutrients such as B vitamins and iron. Brown rice flour can go bad quickly and should be stored in the refrigerator to prolong its shelf life. This flour works beautifully alongside sorghum flour or buckwheat flour in many baked goods and is a top pick for many who bake gluten-free because of its neutral flavor and color.

Superfine Brown Rice Flour

An absolute must for making certain recipes, such as my Simple Homemade Pasta (page 22) and Easygoing Pie Crust (page 34), this flour is brown rice flour that has been double milled to produce a silky texture very similar to that of wheat flour. Sometimes difficult to locate in grocery stores, it can easily be found for purchase online or can often be ordered by local natural foods stores if you ask politely. (This saves on pricey shipping; this flour is heavy!)

Buckwheat Flour

When purchasing buckwheat flour, keep in mind that there are two varieties to choose from: light and dark. Light buckwheat flour has the most neutral flavor, but has less nutritional value than the darker variety. The color of the darker flour is almost grayish brown, producing a more earthy-looking result. The darker variety is what I recommend because it has a wonderful, mild grassy flavor and provides a really great texture in baked goods as well as a good dose of iron, potassium, and omega fatty acids. Even though it sounds like it's a foe to the gluten intolerant, it is completely friendly. It's just a name!

Chickpea Flour

High in protein and folic acid, this flour is made by grinding whole dried chickpeas and is essential in Indian cookery, from thickening sauces and coating fried foods to making certain types of breads. It produces different textures, ranging from eggy to cakey, depending on how you use the flour. It has a light yellow color and silky texture and is also known as besan or gram flour.

Cocoa Powder

Often thought of as just a flavoring for baked goods, cocoa powder actually behaves quite nicely when used as a flour. It soaks up moisture, adds density, and of course, imparts a wonderful chocolate flavor. This is why flourless chocolate cake works so well; it's not actually *flour*less at all! Cocoa powder also boasts a nice nutritional profile that includes calcium, iron, potassium, manganese, and fiber.

Cornmeal

Famous for making cornbread delicious, cornmeal lends a complex texture to baked goods and is a great source of fiber. It works wonderfully as a batter or coating on fried foods as well. Finely ground cornmeal is best for baking, and the coarser grind is more suited to making dishes like polenta, where it has more time to absorb water to make it soft.

Cornstarch

This flour, or starch, is great to use in addition to other gluten-free flours to improve texture. Most commonly thought of as a gravy thickener, cornstarch is also great in baking and cooking. It adds a nice softness and body to breads, cookies, cakes, and more.

Masa Harina

This is a finely ground flour, made from corn treated with food-grade lime and is high in fiber, folic acid, and iron. Traditionally used to make tortillas and tamales, it also works well in baking, adding a nice texture to many treats both sweet and savory.

Millet Flour

Millet is a grass with small seeds that when ground yields a flour that is slightly dry in texture and mild in flavor. It's a good source of protein, calcium, zinc, phosphorous, niacin, and manganese. This flour works great in baked goods when mixed with a moister flour, such as almond meal or chickpea flour.

Potato Flour

Made from the entire potato, potato flour is a perfect addition to gluten-free baked goods, giving a moist and neutral flavor. It is also high in vitamin B6, potassium, and calcium.

Potato Starch

Potato starch is made from only the starchy part of the potato, unlike potato flour, which is made from the entire potato. There is a difference between potato starch and flour in texture as well, with potato starch having less body than potato flour. Potato starch is a popular addition to many gluten-free flour blends because it adds a nice texture to baked goods and is not too sticky and not too dry. It is used similar to cornstarch in baking.

Quinoa Flour

Quinoa is a nifty little grain that has been seeing a lot of love in the mainstream foodie world as of late. This flour is similar to brown rice flour in taste and texture and can vary in color depending on the variety of quinoa grain that is ground to make the flour. A nutritional powerhouse, this flour is an excellent source of protein, fiber, omega-3 and omega-6 fatty acids, iron, copper, manganese, folate, and more!

Did You Know?
One cup (170 g) of quinoa grains has as much protein as a ¼-pound (115 g) hamburger patty ... without all the added fat and cholesterol.

Sorghum Flour

Sorghum is a staple grain in Africa, used in everything from bread to beer making. It is mainly available in two varieties: sweet white and regular sorghum. Regular sorghum tends to be used more as a breakfast cereal grain, and sweet white is very similar in taste and texture to brown rice flour. Sweet white sorghum is my absolute favorite gluten-free flour because of its similarity to wheat flour. It's what I use in my recipes, though either type will work if you can only find regular. It's also rich in phosphorous, iron, fiber, and protein.

Sweet White Rice Flour (Mochiko)

Made from high-starch, short-grain rice, or "sticky" rice, this flour adds a density to baked goods and is used to make Asian treats such as mochi cakes, sticky rice noodles, and clear rice papers. It is not super beneficial nutritionally, but only a small amount is usually needed in most gluten-free mixes. It is similar in function to a starch but also works as binder for doughs or batters that need to be slightly tacky.

Tapioca Starch

Made from the cassava root, this flour, when used in moderation, adds a nice density to batter and dough. When overused, though, it tends to make baked goods gummy. Again, because it is a starch, it's not too high on the nutritional scale, but it does have a bit of iron in it. Be careful when sourcing this flour; I've had brands that smell kinda funky and leave a bad aftertaste with baked goods. The best guideline is that this flour should have practically no smell at all. If it smells like anything, chances are it's no good. Bob's Red Mill brand is always a safe choice if you're not sure which brand to try.

Teff Flour

Teff flour, ground from the teeny tiny teff grain (the smallest in the world, in fact), boasts a ridiculous amount of nutrients, has a mild flavor, and adds the perfect amount of "sponge" to many baked goods. The flour is simply made by grinding the tiny grain into a fine powder. The flour is similar in texture and color to buckwheat flour, whereas the grain resembles tiny pebbles rather than a smooth flour.

Did You Know?
Teff is so small that a single grain of wheat weighs the same amount as approximately 150 teff grains! Its small size doesn't keep it from being packed full of great things, though—it has a good amount of protein, fiber, iron, calcium, niacin, and omega-3 and omega-6 fatty acids.

White Rice Flour

This is a slightly dry flour that works similarly to brown rice flour, but without all the beneficial vitamins and minerals. It's perfect for making very light-colored cakes and cookies when used in combination with other starches or flours.

Xanthan Gum

Although slightly scary sounding, and a little mysterious in nature, xanthan gum is a very useful binder to have on hand for gluten-free baking. It almost acts as a gluten replacement, and a little bit goes a very long way. Typically recipes call for about 1 to 2 teaspoons powder per cake or couple dozen cookies. Xanthan gum is a bacterial-based additive often found in foods such as ice cream, salad dressings, and sauces. It is popular because of its thickening and binding capabilities in such small amounts. Many people also opt to use guar gum 1:1 in place of xanthan, but I find that xanthan gum produces more predictable results.

A Note on Oats

Many people with Celiac disease have issues with oats, whether or not the oats are certified gluten-free. This is due to the protein avenin, which is similar molecularly to the gluten protein. I, like some other celiacs, suffer this fate, so you won't find any recipes in this book that use oats because I can't accurately test them. If you don't have an oat sensitivity, by all means, give certified gluten-free oat flour a whirl because it is an amazing flour to work with. It has a very wheatlike taste and texture and is easy to make by simply running some uncooked oats though a food processor until a fine flour is produced. It is especially fun to experiment with it in recipes that would normally call for all-purpose wheat flour.

VEGAN SUBSTITUTES GUIDE

This is a very basic reference guide for folks new to vegan eating or curious about what can be used in place of typical animal-based ingredients such as eggs and milk. You'll find that I use a lot of these ingredients in this book, but you can use them in your own veganizing adventures, too! Cooking and baking are largely based on chemistry, so consistency, fat, water content, and of course, *flavor* play a big role in making recipes work. Ingredients don't have to come from an animal to make a recipe taste good. Really! Plants offer a variety of wonderful flavors and textures while at the same time providing many nutrients that animal foods lack. One of the best ways to get acquainted with the awesomeness that is vegan cooking is by veganizing your favorite recipes. It's easy and fun! Here's a list of replacements that are usually pretty foolproof when converting recipes.

Egg Substitutes

Apple Cider Vinegar: Use in cakes and muffins; substitute each egg with 1 tablespoon (15 ml) vinegar, added at the end of making your batter. This only works when either baking soda or baking powder is also used in the recipe.

Applesauce: Applesauce adds binding (but not rising) capabilities and a cakelike texture to baked goods. Use ¼ cup (60 g) applesauce per egg in baking recipes.

Banana: One small banana replaces two or three eggs in many baking recipes. It also adds sweetness and moisture to baked goods (but no rising power).

Commercial Egg Replacer (such as EnerG): This stuff generally comes in powdered form and is activated with warm water. It must be mixed before adding to recipes for best results. Generally, about 1½ teaspoons (7 g) mixed with 3 tablespoons (45 ml) warm water equals one egg.

Extra-Firm Tofu: This is excellent for making tofu scrambles and veggie quiche. Drain the tofu well, crumble, season, and sauté in a touch of oil to make a quick and tasty tofu scramble.

Flaxseed Meal: For one "egg," mix 1 tablespoon (15 g) flaxseed meal with 2 tablespoons (30 ml) water and allow to rest for a few minutes. I like this ratio because it makes a thick, rather than watery, egg replacement. The "flax egg" is perfect for using as a binder in recipes, but is not suitable for rising purposes.

Silken Tofu: Use ¼-cup (60 g) blended silken tofu to replace one egg in baking. This is best if used in dense baked goods such as brownies and cheese-cakes. Silken tofu, like regular tofu, is available in different firmnesses, from soft to extra-firm. Extra-firm works best for cooking and eating, and the other varieties work especially well when blended and used in baking.

Milk Substitutes

Almond Milk: Similar to 2 percent milk in taste and texture, this is my favorite nondairy milk to use. It works beautifully in baking and goes great with cookies. See page 18 if you'd like to try making your own.

Coconut Milk: Available canned or refrigerated, coconut milk in a carton (such as So Delicious brand) is mostly reserved for drinking or cereal topping. Canned coconut milk is very similar to heavy whipping cream and can be used as such when cooking and baking. Mixing one can of full-fat milk with equal parts water also makes a bargain "lite" coconut milk!

Hemp Milk: Oftentimes controversial because of its relation to the infamous weed, hemp is actually an amazing plant that can be used to make everything from clothing to food. Hemp milk is great for cooking, baking, and simply drinking. It has a medium-bodied texture and a mild flavor, making it suitable for sweet and savory uses.

Rice Milk: Rice milk is a lighter nondairy milk, similar to skim milk in taste and texture. It makes an excellent light beverage when chilled and is a really great addition to smoothies.

Soymilk: Probably the most well-known of non-dairy milks, soymilk has similar qualities to almond milk, though it does have a slightly "beany" aftertaste.

Cheese Substitutes

Nutritional Yeast: This magical ingredient is a staple in many vegans' pantries. It's a bright yellow, deactivated yeast that is cultured on molasses or sugarcane. Even though it's slightly unheard of outside of the vegan and vegetarian world (though you may have seen at the movie theater, where it is sometimes offered as a popcorn condiment), it is pretty easy to come by in most natural foods stores. Cheesy in flavor and chock-full of vitamins and minerals, nutritional yeast makes a wonderful addition to sauces and baked goods. It also makes a great topping similar to Parmesan cheese.

Store-Bought Nondairy Cheese: The nondairy cheeses that are available nowadays are pretty darn impressive. They melt, they stretch, they come in a variety of flavors … what's not to love? More and more varieties are becoming available on the market, but my personal favorite is Daiya brand shredded cheese, which is made from the amazing cassava root!

Butter Substitutes

Coconut Oil: This fat makes a great natural alternative to margarine or hydrogenated vegetable shortening in many recipes. This oil has a very low melting point of slightly above room temperature, but when chilled in your fridge it becomes a very firm solid similar in texture to cocoa butter, making it a perfect base for no-bake desserts. You can find coconut oil in most supermarkets, either with the Asian ingredients or with the organic groceries.

Nondairy Margarine: This is available in many different brands, and probably the most widely known in the United States is Earth Balance brand nondairy margarine. Use cup for cup like butter when baking and cooking.

Olive Oil: One of my favorite oils to use in a variety of foods, olive oil works beautifully in cooking, baking, and just adding straight to foods to give a light, yet complex flavor. Extra-virgin olive oil is my favorite for baking and cooking because it has the most finely nuanced flavor of all olive oils. The color of extra-virgin can range from a pale greenish to a golden yellow. Generally, the darker the color of the oil, the more pronounced the flavor. Be sure to seek out labels that say "100 percent extra-virgin olive oil," rather than "light" or "light-tasting olive oil," because the latter oils can sometimes contain other ingredients. Virgin olive oil and pure olive oil have less delicate flavors and are good for frying or roasting. You can also purchase unfiltered olive oils that are wonderful for dipping breads and drizzling onto cooked pasta.

Heavy Cream Substitutes

Canned Coconut Milk: Usually found along with Asian foods on your grocery store's shelves, full-fat coconut milk is perfect to use instead of heavy whipping cream. When refrigerated, the solid fat rises to the top of the can and can be skimmed off then whipped just like heavy cream.

Melted Nondairy Ice Cream: This is best reserved for sweet uses, but works beautifully in place of condensed milk or heavy cream for treats like pies and cakes. The flavor combinations are endless here.

Nondairy Creamer: Brands such as Silk and So Delicious have come a long way with coffee creamer. Use it in recipes calling for heavy whipping cream in baking and confection making.

Honey Substitutes

Agave Nectar: Made from the same cactus that tequila comes from, agave is a great substitute for honey because of its intense sweetness and viscous texture. Agave nectar browns up more quickly in baked goods than sugar does, so keep that in mind when using it. Often whatever you are baking will appear to be cooked through because of the color, but it still has a ways to go until done. Agave is my go-to sweetener as a honey substitute because I find it has a mild flavor and just about the same amount of sweetness as the bees' food. Substitute cup for cup for honey.

Brown Rice Syrup: Brown rice syrup is not only a great honey substitute but it's also a great sweetener for teas, hot cereals, and countless other uses. It is fairly mild in flavor and very sticky in texture. Substitute cup for cup for honey.

Maple Syrup: Maple syrup is available in various grades; 100 percent pure maple syrup makes a fragrant and distinctive substitute for honey and can be substituted 1:1.

⟲ Basic Recipes ⟳

In the following pages, you'll find many recipes I rely on every day, such as almond milk and vegetable broth. But I've also included a few that I consider more frivolous recipes, such as a white chocolate baking bar and a flaky pie crust, which are also called for as ingredients in other parts of this book.

ALMOND MILK

Almond milk is my favorite nondairy milk to use in baking, cooking, and just simply drinking. It's available in many supermarkets and natural foods stores, but making your own at home is a cinch and allows you to control exactly what does (and doesn't) go in it. This milk is just as delicious with the sweetener and vanilla left out, if you prefer.

•••••••••••••••• YIELD: ABOUT 7 SERVINGS, ¾ CUP (180 ML) EACH ••••••••••••••••

2 cups (300 g) raw whole almonds, soaked overnight in water to cover

6½ cups (1.5 L) filtered water, divided

⅓ cup (80 ml) agave nectar

2 teaspoons (2 ml) pure vanilla extract

Drain the almonds, and then place in a blender. Add 4½ cups (1,060 ml) of the water, the agave, and the vanilla extract and blend until very smooth, about 4 minutes. Strain through a cheesecloth, and then stir in the remaining 2 cups (470 ml) water. Store in an airtight container in the refrigerator.

RECIPE NOTE

Use the strained pulp to add to smoothies, cookies, cakes, and other recipes. It also makes a delicious addition to Cream of Jasmine Rice (page 62).

NUTRITIONAL ANALYSIS:
SERVING: 103 CALORIES; 9 G FAT; 4 G PROTEIN; 3.3 G CARBOHYDRATE; 2 G DIETARY FIBER; 0 MG CHOLESTEROL.

VEGETABLE BROTH

This simple vegetable broth packs such a great amount of flavor you'll never miss the animal-product-laden versions. It's perfect for freezing in ice cube trays and conveniently using when needed to add a little burst of flavor to stews, sautés, and sauces. Or freeze an entire freezer bag full of broth to have soup stock on hand.

•••••••••••••••••• YIELD: 12 SERVINGS, 1 CUP (235 ML) EACH ••••••••••••••••••

1 Vidalia onion, or about 1 cup (160 g) chopped

1 bunch celery, or about 3 to 4 cups (300 to 400 g) chopped

5 carrots, or about 2 cups (260 g) peeled and chopped

5 or 6 medium-size kale leaves

2 fresh tomatoes

2 cloves garlic, minced (optional)

12 cups (2.9 L) water

Salt to taste

Wash the vegetables and trim away any tough or damaged parts. Parts such as kale stems and celery leaves are great to use, so don't toss those!

Chop the vegetables roughly and place in a stockpot. Add the water and cook over medium-low heat until the veggies are very soft, about 25 to 30 minutes. Let cool until easy to handle.

Strain vegetables through cheesecloth into a large bowl or container. Squeeze the cheesecloth tightly to ensure no broth goes to waste and then discard the cooked veggies. Add salt to taste.

Store in an airtight container in the fridge for up to 3 days or freeze for later use in a freezer-safe container or bag.

RECIPE NOTE

Feel free to use whatever vegetables you have on hand. This recipe is very basic and can be hyped up with the addition of mushrooms, cabbage, corn … you name it! Any combination of vegetables can be used to make a broth, but I find that a good broth should at least contain celery or celeriac; onions, leeks, or shallots; and carrots or parsnips. These ingredients are the crux of great recipes in many different cuisines simply because they taste magnificent when combined.

NUTRITIONAL ANALYSIS

PER SERVING: 30 CALORIES; 0 G FAT; 3 G PROTEIN; 0 G CARBOHYDRATE; 0 G DIETARY FIBER; 0 MG CHOLESTEROL.

SIMPLE HOMEMADE PASTA

A great homemade pasta is something that I usually reserve for special occasions, but since going gluten-free, often just *eating* a good pasta can be a reason to celebrate. This one is my favorite, and it is as basic as it gets for gluten-free pasta.

•   YIELD: 4 SERVINGS   •

2 cups (277 g) superfine brown rice flour (such as Authentic Foods brand), plus more for kneading and rolling

I teaspoon xanthan gum

I teaspoon sea salt

I¼ cups (300 ml) water

Sift together the superfine brown rice flour, xanthan gum, and sea salt in a large bowl. Using a fork, stir in the water a little bit at a time to form a soft dough. Turn out onto a lightly (brown rice) floured surface and knead about 2 to 3 tablespoons (14 to 21 g) flour into the dough until it is no longer sticky. Add just enough to make a slightly elastic dough.

Divide the dough in half. Pat each section with a touch more superfine brown rice flour on each side. Turn one section out onto a lightly floured countertop.

Using a lightly floured rolling pin, roll one section of dough into an 8 x 16-inch (20 x 40 cm) rectangle until the dough is about ⅛-inch (3 mm) thick. If the dough sticks to your rolling surface, add a touch more flour. To get thinner noodles, feel free to roll out between two sheets of plastic wrap, making sure the dough is not sticky before doing so. If needed, transfer sections of the dough to a safe cutting surface so you don't ruin your countertop!

Cut the dough into long noodles, ¼-inch (6 mm) wide and 8-inches (20 cm) long, using a pizza cutter. Individually remove noodles from your rolling surface and delicately place into a loose pile. Repeat with the other section of dough.

Bring at least 8 cups (1.9 L) lightly salted water to a boil in a pot. Once the water is at a rolling boil, drop in one pile of noodles, stirring gently to separate. Let the pasta cook for 3 minutes. Drain and rinse briefly under cold water. Repeat with the other pile of noodles.

Serve with your favorite pasta sauce or simply dress with salt, extra-virgin olive oil, and some freshly chopped herbs.

NUTRITIONAL ANALYSIS

PER SERVING: 215 CALORIES; 2 G FAT; 45 G PROTEIN; 45 G CARBOHYDRATE; 3 G DIETARY FIBER; 0 MG CHOLESTEROL.

BIZQUIX

This is a simple biscuit mix that can be used where most traditional biscuit mixes are called for. Use in pancakes, biscuits (page 43), waffles, and other recipes where you would normally use an all-purpose baking mix.

•••••••••••••••• YIELD: 5½ CUPS (687 G), OR 10 SERVINGS ••••••••••••••••

3 cups (474 g) superfine brown rice flour

1½ cups (195 g) sorghum flour

¾ cup (97 g) potato starch

¼ cup (32 g) tapioca starch

1 teaspoon xanthan gum

½ teaspoon sea salt

1¼ teaspoons (5 g) baking soda

3 tablespoons (21 g) baking powder

1 cup (240 ml) coconut oil, slightly softened but not liquefied

In large bowl combine the brown rice flour, sorghum flour, potato starch, tapioca starch, xanthan gum, sea salt, baking soda, and baking powder.

Stir in the coconut oil and mix with a pastry blender or your hands until crumbly. Cover and chill in the refrigerator for a few hours until cold.

Pulse the crumbly mixture in a food processor until it turns into a very uniform and fine mixture.

Store in an airtight container in the refrigerator for up to three weeks.

RECIPE NOTE

To make a basic pancake recipe, stir together 2 cups (250 g) Bizquix, 1 tablespoon (15 ml) apple cider vinegar, and 1 to 1½ cups (235 to 355 ml) almond milk (page 18). Pour about ¼ cup (60 g) batter onto a hot greased or nonstick griddle. Cook until the edges brown slightly and bubbles form on top, 2 to 3 minutes. Flip the pancake over carefully and continue cooking until the other side is cooked through, 1 to 2 minutes. Top with maple syrup and enjoy!

NUTRITIONAL ANALYSIS

PER SERVING: 369 CALORIES; 20 G FAT; 6 G PROTEIN; 45 G CARBOHYDRATE; 4 G DIETARY FIBER; 0 MG CHOLESTEROL.

BASIC BROWN BREAD

good [handwritten: bad] have had better

This bread is one of my favorites to have around for midday snacking, toasting, or using as bread crumbs. It is delicious toasted and topped with vegan mayonnaise, a fresh garden tomato, and a generous sprinkle of freshly ground black pepper.

•   YIELD: 10 SERVINGS   •

1 tablespoon (7 g) active dry yeast

3 tablespoons (40 g) sugar

1½ cups (355 ml) warm water (110°F [43°C])

1¼ cups (150 g) buckwheat flour

¾ cup (97 g) sorghum flour

1 cup (130 g) potato starch

½ cup (60 g) tapioca starch

2 teaspoons (4 g) xanthan gum

1 teaspoon sea salt

3 tablespoons (45 ml) olive oil

In a large electric mixing bowl, combine the yeast, sugar, and warm water and let proof until foamy, about 10 minutes. Lightly grease an 8 x 4-inch (20 x 10 cm) metal loaf pan.

In separate bowl, stir together the buckwheat flour, sorghum flour, potato starch, tapioca starch, xanthan gum, and sea salt.

Add the olive oil to the yeast and mix well. Slowly incorporate the flour mixture until thoroughly combined. Mix on medium speed for about 1 minute or until the dough becomes sticky.

Spread the dough in the prepared pan. Smooth the top with wet fingertips.

Let it rest in a warm place (the top of an oven preheated to 200°F [95°C] and turned off works well) for about 40 minutes or until the dough has risen a bit.

Preheat the oven to 450°F (230°C, or gas mark 8).

Transfer the pan to the center rack of the oven and bake for 15 minutes.

Reduce the oven temperature to 385°F (195°C, or gas mark 5) and bake for 30 to 35 minutes longer or until golden brown on top and hollow sounding when tapped.

Let the bread cool in the pan for 10 minutes before transferring to a cooling rack, and then let cool completely on the rack before cutting with a serrated knife. Store in an airtight container.

NUTRITIONAL ANALYSIS

PER SERVING: 130 CALORIES; 5 G FAT; 2 G PROTEIN; 22 G CARBOHYDRATE; 2 G DIETARY FIBER; 0 MG CHOLESTEROL.

TOFU FETA

excellent

This stuff isn't *exactly* like feta cheese, but it's pretty close and makes a great addition to salads, pizzas, and hors d'oeuvres. I like mine extra salty, but feel free to adjust to your own taste.

•••••••••••••• YIELD: 10 SERVINGS, ABOUT 2 OUNCES (55 G) EACH ••••••••••••••••

1 block (1 pound, or 454 g) extra-firm tofu, drained and pressed to remove any extra water

3 tablespoons (45 ml) apple cider vinegar

3 tablespoons (45 ml) kalamata or other olive juice (from a jar of olives packed in water, not oil)

6 tablespoons (90 ml) lemon juice

2 to 3 teaspoons (10 to 15 g) sea salt

The night before, freeze the pressed tofu overnight in a freezer-safe plastic bag.

The next day, let the frozen tofu thaw for about 4 hours and then press again to remove any moisture. Crumble into ½-inch (1.3 cm) chunks into a medium-size bowl.

In a separate small bowl, whisk together the apple cider vinegar, olive juice, lemon juice, and 2 teaspoons (10 g) of the sea salt. Drizzle over the tofu and stir to combine.

Let rest in the fridge for 1 hour, stir again, and let rest 1 hour longer. Add the remaining 1 teaspoon (5 g) salt to taste, if desired. Store in an airtight container for up to 1 week.

RECIPE NOTE

Tofu can easily be pressed to remove all water either by using a handy-dandy gadget such as the TofuXpress or by wrapping tightly in several paper towels, placing between two plates, topping with a couple of heavy canned items (two 28-ounce [784 g] cans works well), and allowing to rest for 1 to 2 hours, replacing the paper towels halfway through.

NUTRITIONAL ANALYSIS

PER SERVING: 35 CALORIES; 2 G FAT; 4 G PROTEIN; 2 G CARBOHYDRATE; 0 G DIETARY FIBER; 0 MG CHOLESTEROL.

CASHEW CREAM

This is an incredibly easy and useful recipe that can be used in a variety of dishes, from acting as a delicious condiment to incorporating into recipes such as soups and stews for added creaminess.

•••••••••••••• YIELD: 20 SERVINGS, 2 TABLESPOONS (30 ML) EACH ••••••••••••••••

2 cups (300 g) raw cashews, soaked in 4 cups (940 ml) water for at least 6 hours, then drained

I cup (235 ml) cold water

3 tablespoons (45 ml) lemon juice

2 to 3 teaspoons (9 to 13 g) sugar (optional)

Dash or two of sea salt

Place all the ingredients in a food processor and blend until very smooth, about 5 minutes. The better quality food processor you have, the smoother the cashew cream will get.

Use as an accompaniment to dips, sauces, or desserts, or even as a topping like sour cream.

Store in a tightly sealed container in the refrigerator for up to one week.

NUTRITIONAL ANALYSIS

PER SERVING: 200 CALORIES; 16 G FAT; 5 G PROTEIN; 13 G CARBOHYDRATE; 1 G DIETARY FIBER; 0 MG CHOLESTEROL.

MASHED YUKON GOLDS

For me, a bowl of homemade mashed potatoes is the epitome of comfort food.
This is my favorite way to prepare mashed potatoes—slightly dry,
yet still quite creamy.

•••••••••••••••••••• YIELD: 8 SERVINGS, 1 CUP (225 G) EACH •••••••••••••••••••••

5 pounds (2.3 kg) unpeeled Yukon gold
potatoes

3 tablespoons (42 g) nondairy margarine

1½ teaspoons sea salt

Freshly cracked black pepper to taste

Bring a large stockpot filled halfway with lightly salted water to
a boil.

Scrub the potatoes well and chop into approximately 1-inch
(2.5 cm) pieces. Once the water reaches a full rolling boil, carefully
add the potatoes and allow water to return to a rolling boil.

As soon as the water returns to a boil, begin timing the
potatoes, cooking for 11 to 13 minutes. Reduce the heat slightly
if needed to avoid boiling over.

Check the potatoes at 11 minutes to see if they are easy to
smash with a fork. You should not have to put any pressure on
them to make this happen. You don't want undercooked potatoes
or your mashed potatoes will end up lumpy; it's better to cook
them for the full 13 minutes if you are unsure.

Once they are very fork-tender, drain in a colander and
transfer to an electric mixing bowl. Mix on low speed, combining
with the margarine and salt until blended. Increase the speed
to medium-high and mix until fluffy and smooth. Stir in more
margarine if desired.

Top with freshly cracked black pepper. Serve hot.

RECIPE NOTE

If you don't have an electric mixer, use a potato masher instead.
When you've blended the mashed potatoes with margarine and salt,
use some elbow grease to mix them so they become extra fluffy.

NUTRITIONAL ANALYSIS

PER SERVING: 265 CALORIES; 0.5 G FAT; 7 G PROTEIN; 60 G CARBOHYDRATE; 6 G DIETARY FIBER; 0 MG CHOLESTEROL.

EASYGOING PIE CRUST

Having a really great pie crust recipe is an essential to every baker's repertoire. This is my go-to pie crust, and it works great in both sweet and savory recipes.

•••••••••••••• YIELD: ONE DEEP-DISH PIE CRUST, OR 12 SERVINGS ••••••••••••••••

1¾ cups (277 g) superfine brown rice flour (such as Authentic Foods brand), plus more for kneading and rolling

½ cup (60 g) cornstarch

½ cup (60 g) tapioca starch

1 teaspoon xanthan gum

1 teaspoon baking powder

2½ tablespoons (45 g) sugar

1 cup plus 2 tablespoons (270 g) nondairy margarine, very cold

3 tablespoons (45 ml) apple cider vinegar

½ cup (120 ml) very cold water

Sift together the 1¾ cups (277 g) brown rice flour, cornstarch, tapioca starch, xanthan gum, baking powder, and sugar in a large bowl. Using a pastry blender, cut in the margarine until the mixture is evenly crumbly. Make a well in the center and then add the vinegar and very cold water, stirring together quickly with a fork.

Turn out the dough onto a lightly (brown rice) floured surface and knead in about 1 to 2 tablespoons (7 to 14 g) additional brown rice flour, if necessary, until workable. Do not overknead; a flip or two will do just fine.

Pat into a disk and chill until very cold, about 2 hours in the fridge or 30 minutes in the freezer. The pie crust will be slightly sticky, especially as it returns to room temperature, so rolling between two sheets of parchment or waxed paper is a must.

Use as a crust in your favorite pie recipe following the recipe directions. If the crust needs to be prebaked, bake at 400°F (200°C, or gas mark 6) for about 10 to 15 minutes until lightly golden brown.

RECIPE NOTES

* Double ingredient amounts if making lattice or a double-crust pie.
* If making a savory pie, omit the sugar and add in chopped fresh herbs such as thyme, parsley, or oregano.
* If you don't have a pastry blender, two butter knives work well to "cut" the mixture into crumbles.

NUTRITIONAL ANALYSIS

PER SERVING: 290 CALORIES; 18 G FAT; 2 G PROTEIN; 31 G CARBOHYDRATE; 1 G DIETARY FIBER; 0 MG CHOLESTEROL.

VANILLA BEAN ICE CREAM

Vanilla bean ice cream was always my favorite flavor growing up, and this recipe gives one particular brand I used to love a run for its money. Creamy, rich, and wholeheartedly decadent, you'd never know this was made without dairy.

· · · · · · · · · · · · · · · YIELD: 8 SERVINGS, ½ CUP (100 G) EACH · · · · · · · · · · · · · · ·

2 cans (13.5 ounces, or 378 ml each) full-fat coconut milk

1½ cups (300 g) sugar

2 vanilla bean pods, split lengthwise and seeds scraped

¾ teaspoon sea salt

In a saucepan, combine the coconut milk, sugar, scraped vanilla seeds, and vanilla bean pods. Warm briefly over medium heat until the sugar has dissolved, stirring occasionally, about 2 minutes. Remove the pods from the mixture and add the salt. Pour into a bowl and chill in the fridge for at least 30 minutes or until cold.

Process in an ice cream maker according to the manufacturer's instructions. Once it is finished, place in a flexible airtight container and freeze until firm enough to scoop (this usually takes a couple of hours).

RECIPE NOTE

This recipe also makes a nice base for more exciting flavors. Experiment with mix-ins like bits of cookie dough, fruit, nuts, chocolate chips, chopped dates, cookie bits, candies, vegan marshmallows . . . you name it!

NUTRITIONAL ANALYSIS

PER SERVING: 300 CALORIES; 18 G FAT; 2 G PROTEIN; 34 G CARBOHYDRATE; 2 G DIETARY FIBER; 0 MG CHOLESTEROL.

WHITE CHOCOLATE BAKING BAR

Adapted from an ingenious recipe created by one of my favorite cookbook authors, Hannah Kaminsky, this recipe yields a basic white chocolate bar that's great for baking. Cocoa butter is tough to find in many supermarkets and is best sought out in natural foods stores or online. It is often sold in solid chunks and is very firm (just like a chocolate bar) at room temperature. I included this recipe in my basics section because if there is one confection I love having around, it's white chocolate; short of making your own, a good nondairy variety is hard to come by.

•••••••••••••••••• YIELD: 10 SERVINGS, 1 OUNCE (28 G) EACH ••••••••••••••••••

½ cup plus 2 tablespoons (90 g) confectioners' sugar

3 tablespoons (24 g) soymilk powder

7 ounces (207 g) food-grade cocoa butter, chopped

1 teaspoon vanilla extract

In a small bowl, whisk together the confectioners' sugar and soymilk powder until very well combined.

In the bowl of a double boiler, over medium-low heat, begin to melt the cocoa butter just until part of the mixture starts to become liquefied. Add 1 to 2 tablespoons of the confectioners' sugar and soymilk powder mixture to the melting cocoa butter and stir with a wooden spoon until smooth and once again liquefied.

Repeat this process until all the sugar and soymilk powder has been incorporated with the cocoa butter. The mixture should be liquid once everything is combined. Once all the solid cocoa butter has melted, remove from the heat.

Quickly stir in the vanilla and then transfer the mixture to a large chocolate bar mold or a silicone baking dish. Chill in the refrigerator for 2 hours, or until firm, before using.

Store in an airtight container or plastic bag in the fridge to keep from melting or becoming soft. Use in your favorite recipes where white chocolate is called for. This baking bar keeps for up to 3 months if stored in the refrigerator.

NUTRITIONAL ANALYSIS

PER SERVING: 180 CALORIES; 20 G FAT; 0 G PROTEIN; 0 G CARBOHYDRATE; 0 G DIETARY FIBER; 0 MG CHOLESTEROL.

BREAKFASTS

These recipes will get you up and at 'em and ready to start your day with ingredients like whole grains, fruit, and even chocolate! Many of these recipes are fancy enough to serve to guests if you happen to be hosting a lovely brunch for a few of your friends.

BISCUITS & HERBED COUNTRY GRAVY

Biscuits and gravy has been a staple at my household for years.
This dish is not only perfect for a lazy Sunday afternoon brunch, but it also
makes a wonderful main course when having breakfast for dinner!

• • • • • • • • • • • • • • • • • • • YIELD: 9 BISCUITS, OR SERVINGS •

FOR BISCUITS:

4 cups (500 g) Bizquix (page 20)
1¼ cups plus 2 tablespoons (325 ml) nondairy milk

FOR GRAVY:

¼ cup (32 g) sorghum flour
¼ cup (32 g) millet flour
5 tablespoons (70 g) nondairy margarine
1 tablespoon (2.5 g) minced fresh herbs, such as rosemary, thyme, or sage
3 cups (705 ml) nondairy milk (lightly sweetened and nonflavored is best)
1¼ teaspoons sea salt
½ teaspoon black pepper

TO MAKE THE BISCUITS: Preheat the oven to 400°F (200°C, or gas mark 6).

Mix together the bizquix and nondairy milk until well combined. Use your hands to shape into 9 biscuits, each about 1½ inches (3.8 cm) in diameter, and place onto an ungreased baking sheet.

Bake for 13 to 15 minutes or until lightly golden brown on the edges. Let cool briefly and then use a flat metal spatula to gently remove from the pan.

TO MAKE THE GRAVY: In a medium-size pan, combine the sorghum flour, millet flour, margarine, and herbs and warm over medium heat. Stir to combine as the margarine melts to create a thick roux. This should take about 1 minute to fully combine.

Using a whisk, add the nondairy milk and continue to stir to prevent lumps from forming. Stir in the salt and pepper. Cook over medium to medium-high heat for about 7 minutes or until the gravy becomes thick, stirring constantly.

Serve the gravy over the biscuits while both are hot.

NUTRITIONAL ANALYSIS
PER SERVING: 343 CALORIES; 16 G FAT; 8 G PROTEIN; 40 G CARBOHYDRATE; 2 G DIETARY FIBER; 0 MG CHOLESTEROL.

STRAWBERRY SHORTCAKE MUFFINS

Like quaint little shortcakes with strawberries hiding inside, these muffins aren't overly sweet and make a great breakfast on the go.

1 cup (200 g) sugar

½ cup (120 ml) olive oil

1½ cups (350 ml) nondairy milk

⅓ cup (80 g) strawberry soy yogurt

1 teaspoon sea salt

3½ teaspoons (16 g) baking powder

2 cups (316 g) superfine brown rice flour

¾ cup (97 g) sorghum flour

¾ cup (97 g) potato starch

1 teaspoon xanthan gum

2 cups (340 g) chopped strawberries

Preheat the oven to 375°F (190°C, or gas mark 5) and lightly grease or line 16 muffin cups with paper liners.

In a medium-size bowl, combine the sugar, olive oil, nondairy milk, and yogurt. In a large bowl, combine the salt, baking powder, brown rice flour, sorghum flour, potato starch, and xanthan gum. Fold in the chopped strawberries and stir to coat with the flour mixture. Gradually stir in the wet ingredients until well combined.

Fill the muffin cups with about ⅓ cup (80 g) batter and bake for 22 to 25 minutes or until lightly golden brown on top. Allow to cool for 15 minutes before serving.

NUTRITIONAL ANALYSIS

PER SERVING: 228 CALORIES; 8 G FAT; 3 G PROTEIN; 37 G CARBOHYDRATE; 2 G DIETARY FIBER; 0 MG CHOLESTEROL.

DOUBLE-CHOCOLATE MUFFINS

These are great for breakfast, but equally as good if eaten as a dessert. Teff flour adds a nutritional boost to these moist and almost brownie-like breakfast muffins.

• • • • • • • • • • • • • • • • • • • YIELD: 15 MUFFINS, OR SERVINGS • • • • • • • • • • • • • • • • • • •

1 cup (130 g) brown rice flour

¼ cup (32 g) tapioca starch

½ cup (65 g) cornstarch

½ cup (65 g) teff flour

½ cup (40 g) cocoa powder

1 teaspoon xanthan gum

½ teaspoon baking soda

2 teaspoons (4 g) baking powder

½ teaspoon sea salt

1⅓ cups (265 g) sugar

2 tablespoons (30 ml) extra-virgin olive oil

1½ cups (350 ml) nondairy milk

2 tablespoons (30 ml) apple cider vinegar

1 teaspoon almond or vanilla extract

1 cup (183 g) nondairy chocolate chips

½ cup (74 g) crushed walnuts

Preheat the oven to 350°F (180°C, or gas mark 4). Line 15 cups of standard-size muffin pans with liners or grease and lightly dust with brown rice flour.

In a medium-size mixing bowl, sift together the brown rice flour, tapioca starch, cornstarch, teff flour, cocoa powder, xanthan, baking soda, baking powder, salt, and sugar until well blended. Make a well in the center of the dry ingredients and then stir in the olive oil, nondairy milk, vinegar, and almond extract. Mix vigorously until very smooth. Stir in the chocolate chips.

Fill the muffin cups about two-thirds full and top with the walnuts. Bake for about 25 minutes or until slightly risen and firm to the touch.

NUTRITIONAL ANALYSIS

PER SERVING: 160 CALORIES; 3 G FAT; 2 G PROTEIN; 34 G CARBOHYDRATE; 2 G DIETARY FIBER; 0 MG CHOLESTEROL.

BLUEBERRY CAKE DONUTS

Just because these donuts are vegan and gluten-free doesn't mean they are anything but delicious donutty goodness. The addition of fresh blueberries makes these an extra-special breakfast-time treat.

••••••••••••••• Yield: 12 donuts and donut holes, or 12 servings ••••••••••••••

For Donuts:

2¼ cups (292 g) sorghum flour

1½ cups (237 g) brown rice flour

¾ cup (97 g) potato starch

¼ cup (32 g) tapioca starch

1 teaspoon xanthan gum

4 teaspoons (8 g) baking powder

¾ teaspoon sea salt

1 cup (225 g) packed brown sugar

3 tablespoons (42 g) nondairy margarine

2 tablespoons (14 g) flaxseed meal mixed with ¼ cup (60 ml) warm water

1 teaspoon vanilla extract

½ cup (115 g) coconut cream (thickest part of coconut milk) or nondairy sour cream

1 cup (245 g) natural applesauce

1 cup (145 g) fresh blueberries

Vegetable oil, for frying

For Glaze:

1 cup (120 g) confectioners' sugar

1 tablespoon (15 ml) nondairy milk

½ teaspoon lemon extract

To make the donuts: In a medium-size bowl, sift together the sorghum flour, brown rice flour, potato starch, tapioca starch, xanthan gum, baking powder, and salt.

In a large mixing bowl, cream together the brown sugar and margarine until smooth. Add the prepared flaxseed meal, vanilla extract, coconut cream, and applesauce. Fold in the blueberries and mix well, being careful not to break them up too much.

Gradually add in the flour mixture and stir well. The dough will be somewhat sticky. Chill for at least 1 hour.

Pour the oil to a depth of 5 inches (13 cm) into a deep fryer and preheat to 365°F (185°C).

Turn the dough out onto a lightly floured surface, adding just enough sorghum to make the dough workable, but still soft. Flatten gently using lightly floured hands to make a patty 1 to 1½ inches (2.5 to 3.8 cm)-thick.

Using two circular cookie cutters (one 3 inches [7.5 cm] and one ¾ inch [2 cm] across. Cut out twelve of the bigger circles and then use the smaller cutter to cut out the middles. Reserve the middles for frying into donut holes.

Carefully drop a few donuts into the hot oil and fry for 3 minutes. Using a slotted metal spoon, remove the donuts from the hot oil and place on a paper bag or paper towels to absorb any excess oil. Return the oil to temperature and repeat until all the donuts have been fried. Cook all donut holes at once for 3 minutes. Let cool.

To make the glaze: Whisk all the ingredients together until very smooth.

Once cooled, place donuts on a wire rack (with a baking sheet underneath to catch any drips) and drizzle with the glaze. Let rest for about 1 hour or until the glaze has hardened.

Nutritional Analysis

Per serving: 260 calories; 20 g fat; 5 g protein; 52 g carbohydrate; 4 g dietary fiber; 0 mg cholesterol.

APPLE CINNAMON BLINTZES

These tender crêpes, which are stuffed with a thick cashew cream and topped with warm cinnamon apples, are a sure-fire way to bring folks together over brunch. Pair with a mug of coffee or a tall glass of orange juice.

••••••••••••••••••••• YIELD: 8 BLINTZES, OR SERVINGS •••••••••••••••••••••

For Crêpes:

3 tablespoons (42 g) sugar

⅔ cup (87 g) cornstarch

⅓ cup (43 g) sorghum flour

⅓ cup (80 g) firm silken tofu

1 cup (240 ml) nondairy milk

1 teaspoon vanilla extract

½ teaspoon sea salt

For Filling:

1 recipe Cashew Cream (page 30)

For Topping:

3 Granny Smith apples, peeled, cored, and thinly sliced

Dash of salt

1 teaspoon cinnamon

2 tablespoons (30 ml) plus ½ cup (120 ml) water, divided

2 tablespoons (28 g) sugar

1 teaspoon cornstarch mixed with 1 tablespoon (15 ml) cold water

To make the crêpes: Add all the ingredients to a blender and process until smooth. Transfer the mixture to a bowl. Cover and refrigerate for at least 1 hour and up to overnight.

To make the topping: Combine the sliced apples, salt, cinnamon, 2 tablespoons (30 ml) water, and sugar in a medium-size bowl. Transfer to a well-seasoned cast-iron or nonstick pan. Cover and cook over medium heat for 7 minutes until the apples are soft.

Add the remaining ½ cup (120 ml) water and cornstarch slurry to the cooked apples and continue to cook over medium heat until thick, about 6 to 8 minutes, stirring occasionally. Remove from the heat and set aside.

To prepare the crêpes, place a crêpe pan or skillet over medium-high heat. Evenly grease with about ½ teaspoon margarine or coconut oil.

Pour ⅓ cup (80 g) batter into the hot pan and gently swirl the pan around in a circular motion to coat with a thin layer of batter. Cook for about 2 minutes and then flip gently using a flat, sturdy spatula; they should be fairly easy to flip if they are done. Cook the other side for approximately 1 minute or until golden on both sides. Place each crêpe on a plate as they are cooked and cover to keep warm. You will get about 8 crêpes from this amount of batter.

To Assemble: Fill the middle of each crêpe with about ¼ cup (50 g) of the cashew cream. Fold the crêpe over twice as you would fold a letter and top with 1 to 2 tablespoons (15 to 30 g) of the cooked apples. Serve warm.

Nutritional Analysis

Per serving: 308 calories; 17 g fat; 7 g protein; 36 g carbohydrate; 1.8 g dietary fiber; 0 mg cholesterol.

CHERRY VANILLA BEAN PANCAKES

Fragrant and flavorful, these pancakes are a delicious start to the morning. Fluffy and laced with vanilla beans and cherries, they really don't need any syrup at all.

• • • • • • • • • • • • • • • • • • • YIELD: ABOUT 7 PANCAKES, OR SERVINGS • • • • • • • • • • • • • • • • •

1¼ cups (162 g) sorghum flour

¼ cup (32 g) tapioca starch

¼ cup (50 g) sugar

½ teaspoon xanthan gum

2 teaspoons (9 g) baking powder

½ teaspoon sea salt

1½ cups (350 ml) nondairy milk

1 tablespoon (15 ml) apple cider vinegar

3 tablespoons (45 ml) olive oil

2 teaspoons (10 g) vanilla bean paste or 2 scraped vanilla beans

¾ cup (117 g) pitted and chopped fresh cherries

Nondairy margarine, for cooking

In a large mixing bowl, sift together the sorghum flour, tapioca starch, sugar, xanthan gum, baking powder, and salt. Next, stir in the nondairy milk, apple cider vinegar, olive oil, and vanilla bean paste to combine. Fold in the chopped cherries.

Preheat a well-seasoned cast-iron or nonstick skillet over medium-low heat and place about ½ teaspoon margarine in the hot skillet to melt. Drop ¼ cup (60 ml) pancake batter evenly onto the preheated pan and cook for about 3 minutes, without touching, until little holes form on top of the pancake. Using a very flat spatula, flip over carefully and cook on the other side for 1 to 2 minutes, or until no batter remains visibly wet from the sides. Transfer to a plate.

Repeat until all the batter has been used; you should get about 7 pancakes. Serve hot.

NUTRITIONAL ANALYSIS

PER SERVING: 262 CALORIES; 8 G FAT; 4 G PROTEIN; 42 G CARBOHYDRATE; 2 G DIETARY FIBER; 0 MG CHOLESTEROL.

CRANBERRY SPICE BAGELS

Here is an easy breakfast treat that is great to make ahead and freeze for later. Like gluten-filled bagels, these are best eaten toasted and slathered with your favorite bagel topper.

• YIELD: 8 BAGELS, OR SERVINGS •

FOR WET INGREDIENTS:

1 tablespoon (7 g) active dry yeast

¼ cup (50 g) sugar

1 cup (235 ml) warm water

½ cup (125 g) natural applesauce

2 tablespoons (30 ml) olive oil

1 tablespoon (15 ml) apple cider vinegar

3 tablespoons (21 g) flaxseed meal mixed with 6 tablespoons (90 ml) warm water

¾ cup (90 g) dried cranberries

FOR DRY INGREDIENTS:

1½ cups (180 g) buckwheat flour

½ cup (65 g) teff flour

1 cup (130 g) sorghum flour

1 cup (130 g) cornstarch

½ cup (65 g) tapioca starch

2 teaspoons (6 g) xanthan gum

½ teaspoon ground nutmeg

¼ teaspoon ground cloves

2 teaspoons (6 g) orange zest

1 teaspoon sea salt

½ cup (65 g) additional sorghum or buckwheat flour

Cornmeal, for dusting baking sheet

Granulated sugar, for dusting

TO PREPARE THE WET INGREDIENTS: In a large bowl, combine the yeast, sugar, and warm water and proof until foamy, about 10 minutes. Add in the applesauce, olive oil, vinegar, prepared flaxseed meal, and cranberries. Mix well.

TO PREPARE THE DRY INGREDIENTS: In a separate bowl, sift together the buckwheat flour, teff flour, sorghum flour, cornstarch, tapioca starch, xanthan, nutmeg, cloves, orange zest, and salt.

Gradually add the dry ingredients to the wet, about ½ cup (65 g) at a time, until well incorporated. Mix vigorously until the dough is sticky. Scrape the sides of the bowl and gather the dough into a tacky ball. Sprinkle in about ¼ cup (30 g) of the additional sorghum flour to make the dough workable, knead the dough briefly, and then add as much as needed of the remaining ¼ cup (30 g) sorghum flour until the dough is easy to handle. Don't go overboard with adding flour, or you'll end up with dry bagels!

Divide the dough into 8 equal size balls. Flatten with floured hands to about 1¾ inches (4.5 cm) thick. Using your finger, poke a hole in the center to form a bagel shape. Repeat until all the dough has been shaped. Smooth the tops and sides with wet fingers to make a uniform shape. Let the bagels rest for about 25 minutes.

Meanwhile, preheat the oven to 375°F (190°C, or gas mark 5). Sprinkle a baking sheet with the cornmeal.

Bring a large pot of water to a boil and drop 1 or 2 bagels at a time into the boiling water. Boil for 2 minutes. Remove with a slotted spoon and place on a wire rack until nearly dry.

Transfer the bagels to the prepared baking sheet and sprinkle the tops of the barely wet bagels with the sugar. Bake for 30 minutes or until golden brown on the edges. Let cool, slice, and serve toasted with your favorite bagel toppings.

NUTRITIONAL ANALYSIS

PER SERVING: 240 CALORIES; 6 G FAT; 5 G PROTEIN; 45 G CARBOHYDRATE; 5 G DIETARY FIBER; 0 MG CHOLESTEROL.

BANANA BREAD SCONES

These scones are like little personal banana breads and are sure to impress any guest. They smell heavenly when baking in the oven and taste amazing served warm.

Good, I'd make again.

•••••••••••••••••• YIELD: 10 SCONES, OR SERVINGS ••••••••••••••••••

- 1 tablespoon (14 g) flaxseed meal mixed with 2 tablespoons (30 ml) warm water
- ¾ cup (173 g) sugar, plus more for sprinkling
- 3 very ripe medium bananas, about 2 cups (300 g) mashed
- 1 teaspoon vanilla extract
- 1 teaspoon sea salt
- ¼ teaspoon ground cloves
- 1 teaspoon cinnamon
- ¼ teaspoon cardamom
- 1 teaspoon baking powder
- 1 teaspoon baking soda
- 1 teaspoon xanthan gum
- 1⅓ cups (173 g) sorghum flour
- 1⅓ cups (173 g) buckwheat flour
- 1 cup (130 g) potato starch
- 1 cup (120 g) walnuts pieces (optional)

Preheat the oven to 400°F (200°C, or gas mark 6). Line a baking sheet with parchment paper or a silicone mat.

In a large mixing bowl, combine the prepared flaxseed meal, sugar, bananas, and vanilla extract. Stir until smooth.

In a separate medium-size bowl, sift together the salt, cloves, cinnamon, cardamom, baking powder, baking soda, xanthan gum, sorghum flour, buckwheat flour, and potato starch.

Slowly add the dry ingredients to the wet and stir until well incorporated. Fold in the walnuts.

Drop the batter by heaping ¼-cup (60 g) portions onto the prepared baking sheet, placing each about 2 inches (5 cm) apart. Sprinkle lightly with additional sugar. You should have 10 scones.

Bake for 15 minutes or until the bottoms are dark golden brown. These are best if eaten fresh from the oven while still a touch warm.

NUTRITIONAL ANALYSIS

PER SERVING: 150 CALORIES; 1 G FAT; 3 G PROTEIN; 35 G CARBOHYDRATE; 3 G DIETARY FIBER; 0 MG CHOLESTEROL.

OLIVE & TOFU FETA TARTLETS

These salty, savory tartlets make a delicious brunch treat to share with friends and loved ones. They are best served warm from the oven.

•   YIELD: 16 TARTLETS, OR SERVINGS   •

FOR CRUST:

1 recipe Easygoing Pie Crust (page 34)

FOR FILLING:

1 cup (145 g) raw cashews, soaked in 1 cup (235 ml) water for at least 1 hour

2 tablespoons (30 ml) water

1 tablespoon (7 g) flaxseed meal mixed with 2 tablespoons (30 ml) warm water

1½ cups (180 g) assorted coarsely chopped olives (kalamata, green, or black, or a mix)

1⅓ cups (300 g) Tofu Feta (page 29)

TO PREPARE THE CRUST: Preheat the oven to 400°F (200°C, or gas mark 6).

Roll out the crust between 2 sheets of parchment paper or on top of a silicone mat until about ¼ inch (6 mm) thick. Cut the dough into 2-inch (5 cm) squares and carefully press into sixteen 2-inch (5-cm) tart pans or standard-size muffin cups. Use a flat metal spatula to help transfer the dough, if necessary. Bake for 10 to 12 minutes until light golden brown. Remove from the oven and reduce the temperature to 350°F (180°C, or gas mark 4).

TO MAKE THE FILLING: Drain the cashews and combine with the water and prepared flaxseed meal in a food processor. Blend until smooth, scraping down the sides as necessary.

Stir the mixture together with the tofu feta and spoon 1 cup (120 g) of the olives and 1 cup (225 g) of the feta into the tart shells, dividing evenly among the cups. Using the back of a spoon, spread the mixture evenly to fill the tart shell. Top each with a sprinkling of the remaining ½ cup (60 g) chopped olives and ⅓ cup (68 g) tofu feta.

Bake for 30 minutes or until the crust edges are golden brown and the olives on top soften and get crispy around the edges. Let the tarts cool for about 15 minutes and then gently remove from the pans. Serve slightly warm.

NUTRITIONAL ANALYSIS

PER SERVING: 200 CALORIES; 7 G FAT; 5 G PROTEIN; 30 G CARBOHYDRATE; 2 G DIETARY FIBER; 0 MG CHOLESTEROL.

BUTTER PECAN STICKY ROLLS

These are similar to cinnamon rolls in texture, but with the addition of buttery pecans. These are best eaten warm from the oven while the icing is still gooey.

FOR ROLLS:

2 tablespoons (14 g) active dry yeast

1 cup (235 ml) almond milk, warmed to about 110°F (43°C)

¾ cup (150 g) sugar, divided

¼ cup (60 ml) olive oil

1 teaspoon vanilla extract or rum extract

¼ cup (32 g) brown rice flour

½ cup (65 g) sorghum flour

¾ cup (97 g) tapioca starch

½ cup (65 g) cornstarch

½ teaspoon baking soda

2 teaspoons (6 g) baking powder

2 teaspoons xanthan gum

½ teaspoon salt

¼ cup (60 g) nondairy margarine, melted

¾ cup (170 g) packed brown sugar

1 cup (110 g) chopped pecans, toasted for about 5 minutes at 400°F (200°C, or gas mark 6)

FOR ICING:

2 cups (240 g) confectioners' sugar

2 tablespoons (30 g) nondairy margarine, slightly softened

1 teaspoon vanilla extract

2 tablespoon (30 ml) almond milk

To MAKE THE ROLLS: In a large bowl, combine the yeast, almond milk, and ¼ cup (50 g) of the sugar and proof until foamy, about 10 minutes. Stir in the olive oil, ½ cup (120 g) sugar, and vanilla extract.

In a separate bowl, sift together the flours, cornstarch, baking soda, baking powder, xanthan, and salt. Gradually stir the dry mixture into the wet until a very sticky dough is formed.

Tape a 25-inch (63.5 cm)-long sheet of plastic wrap to your countertop. Place the dough in the center and top carefully with a second piece of plastic wrap. Roll out into a 20 x 12-inch (51 x 30.5 cm) rectangle. Remove the top layer of plastic wrap.

Lightly brush the melted margarine onto the dough, covering evenly with a thin layer. Sprinkle on an even layer of brown sugar and chopped pecans.

Using the plastic wrap as a guide, roll up the dough tightly, starting with shortest side of the rectangle. Hold the plastic wrap taut as you lift up so that gravity helps roll up the dough. Discard the plastic wrap and cut the rolled dough into eight 2-inch (5 cm) sections; using a flat spatula, gently transfer the rolls into an 8-inch (20 cm) cake pan, individually placing each roll so that they fit snugly in the pan. Cover with a lightly greased sheet of plastic wrap and let rise in a warm place for 45 minutes.

Meanwhile, preheat the oven to 350°F (180°C, or gas mark 4).

Transfer the rolls to the center rack and bake for about 30 minutes, or until the tops are golden brown.

To MAKE THE ICING: Stir the icing ingredients together until smooth and spread or pipe over the warm rolls while they are still in the pan.

Serve warm or at room temperature.

NUTRITIONAL ANALYSIS

PER SERVING: 360 CALORIES; 30 G FAT; 3 G PROTEIN; 30 G CARBOHYDRATE; 3 G DIETARY FIBER; 0 MG CHOLESTEROL.

CREAM OF JASMINE RICE

I cannot think of a breakfast food I enjoyed as often as cream of wheat when I was growing up. It had everything I ever wanted to satisfy my early morning needs, and I loved it so much that I even ate it quite often as a snack. This hot cereal is made with rice, but it has the same nostalgic feel as the kind made with wheat. I learned this technique from Jera, the author of many recipes and tips geared toward the vegan community.

•••••••••••••••••••••••••••• YIELD: 6 SERVINGS ••••••••••••••••••••••••••••

1 cup (195 g) white jasmine rice
5½ cups (1.3 L) water, divided
Dash or two of salt
Brown sugar, for topping
Fresh fruit, for topping

Preheat the oven to 375°F (190°C, or gas mark 5).

Spread the rice evenly onto an ungreased baking sheet. Bake for 10 to 15 minutes, stirring occasionally, until the rice turns golden brown. Remove from the oven and let cool. Grind the rice in a clean coffee grinder or spice grinder, in batches if necessary, until the rice is ground up into small granules.

Mix the ground toasted rice with 1 cup (235 ml) of the water and let rest while you bring the remaining 4½ cups (1 L) water to a boil. Slowly add the rice mixture to the boiling water and reduce the heat to medium-low. Cover and cook until the water has been absorbed and the rice is tender, about 8 minutes. Serve with brown sugar to taste and top with fresh fruit. Serve hot.

RECIPE NOTE

Using a nondairy milk such as almond or coconut milk in place of half of the water called for will make an even creamier breakfast treat.

NUTRITIONAL ANALYSIS

PER SERVING: 107 CALORIES; 0 G FAT; 2 G PROTEIN; 24 G CARBOHYDRATE; 1 G DIETARY FIBER; 0 MG CHOLESTEROL.

{ Chapter 3 }

MAIN COURSES

These hearty main meals are an excellent centerpiece for a delightful dinner or a really filling lunch. Play around with different menu pairings with the soups and sides found in this book. One of my favorite suggestions is trying the Stuffed Cabbage Rolls (page 70) served over some Mashed Yukon Golds (page 33).

POTATO DOSA

Dosa is a filled thin crêpe eaten in southern India and is quickly gaining popularity in the United States, with carts and restaurants dedicated to it popping up everywhere. Even though this recipe takes three days to make, don't be too intimidated because it's mostly in the prep time. You can find all of the ingredients called for here at Indian markets. The chaat masala can be substituted with garam masala if you already have it on hand.

•   YIELD: 6 DOSAS, OR SERVINGS   •

For Dosa Batter:

¾ cup (140 g) urad dal (split white lentils), soaked overnight and drained

4 cups (940 ml) water, divided

1 teaspoon ground coriander powder

¼ teaspoon black pepper

¾ teaspoon sea salt

1 cup (158 g) white rice flour

1¼ cups (198 g) brown rice flour

For Filling:

3 large thin-skinned potatoes, unpeeled, chopped into small pieces

2 leeks (white and light green part only), cleaned well and thinly sliced

1 teaspoon fenugreek powder

½ teaspoon chaat masala

2 tablespoons (30 ml) water

1 medium-size tomato, diced

1 cup (130 g) frozen green peas

¼ teaspoon tamarind concentrate

½ teaspoon turmeric

1 cup (16 g) chopped fresh cilantro

Salt to taste

TO MAKE THE DOSA BATTER: Place the soaked urad dal and 1 tablespoon (15 ml) of the water in a food processor. Blend until a thick fluffy paste is formed, at least 5 minutes.

Transfer the paste to a large mixing bowl and stir in the coriander, black pepper, and salt. Slowly add the remaining water and rice flours and stir until well incorporated into a smooth batter. Cover with light towel and let rest in a warm area for 8 hours. After fermentation, the batter should thicken slightly, with a consistency similar to heavy cream.

TO MAKE THE FILLING: Place the potatoes, leeks, fenugreek powder, chaat masala, and water in a large heavy saucepan. Cover and cook over medium heat for about 15 minutes, or until the potatoes begin to soften. Add the chopped tomato and cook 10 minutes longer. Add the peas and cook just until heated through. Remove from the heat. Stir in the tamarind concentrate, turmeric, cilantro, and salt to taste. Set aside.

Warm a large well-seasoned or nonstick skillet, griddle, or crêpe pan over medium-high heat.

Oil the griddle lightly and use a metal ladle to drop ½ cup (120 ml) of batter onto the hot griddle and immediately spread in a circular motion with the bottom of the ladle to disperse the batter into a thin pancake. Cook for 2 minutes or until golden brown on the bottom.

Once the dosa is golden brown, spread ¼ cup (56 g) of the filling in the center of the pancake (as though you were filling up a burrito) while still on the griddle and fold over one-third of the dosa. Fold over again to close. Remove from the heat and keep warm.

NUTRITIONAL ANALYSIS

PER SERVING: 382 CALORIES; 2 G FAT; 14 G PROTEIN; 79 G CARBOHYDRATE; 14 G DIETARY FIBER; 0 MG CHOLESTEROL.

COLD
SESAME NOODLES

Inspired by a favorite dish often found in Chinese restaurants, these noodles are best when dressed with sauce and eaten immediately because the sauce soaks into the noodles so quickly. If you'd like to make ahead of time, simply store the sauce and noodles separately and combine just before serving.

•   YIELD: 6 SERVINGS   •

16 ounces mỹ tho noodles (flat, wide Asian rice noodles) or other long, wide rice noodles

2 cubes (2 teaspoons) vegetable bouillon

2 tablespoons Bragg's liquid aminos, plus extra to douse noodles

2 tablespoons (32 g) smooth peanut butter

3 tablespoons (45 ml) toasted sesame oil

2 tablespoons (30 ml) agave nectar

½ teaspoon turmeric

1 teaspoon cumin

1 teaspoon Chinese five-spice powder

1 teaspoon freshly grated ginger

¼ cup (25 g) chopped scallion, for garnish

Toasted black sesame seeds, for garnish

Chili garlic sauce, such as Sriracha, for serving

Cook the noodles according to the package directions, dissolving the bouillon cubes in the cooking water first. Once cooked, transfer the noodles to a colander and toss with cold water until they are easy to handle and any extra starch has been rinsed away. Drain well and liberally toss with Bragg's liquid aminos, covering evenly until the noodles appear a golden brown all over.

In a separate bowl, combine the peanut butter and sesame oil and stir until smooth. Stir in the 2 tablespoons (30 ml) Bragg's, agave, turmeric, cumin, and ginger. Pour over the noodles and toss until they are completely covered with a thin layer of sauce.

Garnish with scallion and sesame seeds. You can add the hot sauce on top, stir it in to taste, or pass at the table. Refrigerate for about 30 minutes before serving, tossing occasionally to keep moist. Serve cold.

NUTRITIONAL ANALYSIS

PER SERVING: 105 CALORIES; 1 G FAT; 1 G PROTEIN; 22 G CARBOHYDRATE; 1 G DIETARY FIBER; 0 MG CHOLESTEROL.

STUFFED CABBAGE ROLLS

With a heavy dose of Polish in my lineage, I was lucky enough to be able to feast on cabbage rolls quite often as a child. When I went vegan, I quickly adapted my mother's recipe so that my own family could enjoy them as well.

• • • • • • • • • • • • • • • •   YIELD: 12 CABBAGE ROLLS, OR SERVINGS   • • • • • • • • • • • • • • • •

FOR SAUCE:

2 tablespoons (30 ml) olive oil

2 cloves garlic, minced

1 Vidalia onion, diced

1½ teaspoons sea salt, divided

3 cans (6 ounces, or 170 g each) tomato paste

1¾ cups (420 ml) water

3 tablespoons (40 g) sugar

FOR FILLING:

1 cup (235 ml) water

1 cube (1 teaspoon) vegetable bouillon

1 cup (100 g) textured vegetable protein (TVP)

2 tablespoons (8 g) minced fresh oregano

1 tablespoon (2.5 g) minced fresh basil

2 cups (330 g) cooked brown rice (cooked in vegetable broth or veggie bouillon–infused water)

1 large head green cabbage

Preheat the oven to 325°F (170°C, or gas mark 3).

TO MAKE THE SAUCE: Heat the olive oil in a skillet over medium heat, add the garlic and onion, sprinkle with 1 teaspoon of the salt, and sauté until the onion becomes caramelized, 6 to 8 minutes. Add the tomato paste, water, sugar, and remaining ½ teaspoon salt and stir until smooth. Simmer on low for about 5 minutes, stirring occasionally, and then remove from the heat.

TO MAKE THE FILLING: In a small saucepan, bring the water and bouillon cube to a boil. Toss the textured vegetable protein with the oregano and basil in a heat-safe bowl. Pour the boiling water over the TVP. Cover and let rest for about 5 minutes or until all the water has been absorbed. Fluff with a fork. Combine the TVP with the brown rice in a medium-size bowl.

To assemble, cut off the bottom of the head of cabbage and discard the two outermost leaves. Slice off a bit more of the bottom where the leaves join. Ensure that you have 12 solid, unbroken cabbage leaves.

Cover the bottom of a deep 9 x 13-inch (23 x 33 cm) baking dish with some sauce.

Place about ⅓ cup (57 g) of the filling in the center of a cabbage leaf and fold each side over to shape into a rectangular pouch. Place in the pan with the folded side down to hold in place. Repeat until all the rolls have been made and then generously cover with the remaining sauce. Cover with foil.

Bake for 1 hour and 15 minutes or until the cabbage is soft when pierced with a fork. Serve warm.

NUTRITIONAL ANALYSIS

PER SERVING: 200 CALORIES; 3 G FAT; 5 G PROTEIN; 40 G CARBOHYDRATE; 4 G DIETARY FIBER; 0 MG CHOLESTEROL.

SLOW-SIMMERED TOFU WITH PEANUT SAUCE

This savory tofu dish requires a little forethought because you need to freeze the tofu overnight and simmer the dish for some time, but it's well worth it. The peanut sauce lends just the right amount of sweetness to the dish and is also great served over basmati rice or quinoa.

•••••••••••••••••••••••• YIELD: 4 SERVINGS ••••••••••••••••••••••••

- 1 block (15 ounces, or 425 g) extra-firm tofu
- 5 carrots, peeled and sliced
- 2 cans (13.5 ounces, or 378 g each) full-fat coconut milk
- 1 medium-size Spanish onion, diced
- 2 cloves garlic, minced
- 1 teaspoon freshly grated ginger
- 3 bay leaves
- ¼ cup (65 g) creamy peanut butter
- ⅛ teaspoon mombasa powder, or ¼ teaspoon cayenne pepper
- Salt to taste
- Cooked basmati rice, for serving

RECIPE NOTE

Mombasa is a chile pepper (in the cayenne family) that packs a lot of heat! It is said to be one of the hottest spices available and is often used in African cuisine. It is not all that common and is usually found only in specialty spice stores. Cayenne pepper can be substituted in place, just double the amount!

The night before you begin, drain and press the tofu (see Tofu Feta, page 29), cut into 4 equal pieces, and seal tightly in a freezer-safe plastic bag. Freeze overnight.

The next day, in a large, heavy skillet, stir together the sliced carrots, coconut milk, onion, garlic, ginger, bay leaves, peanut butter, and mombasa. Place the frozen tofu cutlets (no need to thaw) in the pan, shimmying the tofu down into the coconut mixture while gently guiding the veggies to the sides of the tofu, so that the cutlets lie flat in the pan.

Cook over medium heat until the sauce begins to boil, about 15 minutes. Cover, reduce the heat to medium-low, and simmer for about 2 hours, spooning sauce on top of the tofu every once in a while. During the duration of the cooking time, do not flip over the cutlets! You want them to get nice and caramelized on the bottom side, so let them stay right where they are the entire cooking time. Stir the sauce occasionally.

Uncover the pan and cook for 1 hour longer or until the sauce has reduced to a thick, gravy-like consistency and the edges of the carrots and onions are golden brown. The total cooking time is 3 hours. Remove the bay leaves and serve over some fluffy basmati rice.

NUTRITIONAL ANALYSIS

PER SERVING: 215 CALORIES; 13 G FAT; 14 G PROTEIN; 16 G CARBOHYDRATE; 5 G DIETARY FIBER; 0 MG CHOLESTEROL.

SPICY GOULASH

This spicy noodle dish is a fun twist on a common dinner we often make at the Kramer household. It's also one of the best ways I've found to highlight the awesomeness that is Soyrizo.

16 ounces (454 g) brown rice elbow noodles

1 tablespoon (15 ml) olive oil, plus more for drizzling

1 teaspoon sea salt, plus more for sprinkling

2 cups (300 g) chopped green bell pepper

1 Vidalia onion, diced

2 cloves garlic, minced

1 tablespoon (4 g) minced fresh oregano

1 tablespoon (2.5 g) minced fresh sage

1½ teaspoons fennel seeds

1 can (28 ounces, or 794 g) diced tomatoes (do not drain)

12 ounces (340 g) Soyrizo

1 to 2 teaspoons crushed red pepper flakes

¼ teaspoon dried marjoram

⅔ cup (86 g) nutritional yeast

Cook the pasta according to package directions. Drain and then drizzle with olive oil and salt lightly. Set aside.

In a large frying pan, heat the 1 tablespoon (15 ml) oil and sauté the bell pepper, onion, garlic, oregano, sage, and fennel seeds until the vegetables are tender, about 10 minutes.

Stir in the diced tomatoes, Soyrizo, red pepper flakes, 1 teaspoon sea salt, marjoram, and nutritional yeast. Let the sauce simmer for about 5 minutes and then toss with the pasta.

Serve hot.

NUTRITIONAL ANALYSIS

PER SERVING: 396 CALORIES; 6 G FAT; 15 G PROTEIN; 75 G CARBOHYDRATE; 10 G DIETARY FIBER; 0 MG CHOLESTEROL.

DELI-STYLE CHICKPEA SALAD

I believe the world cannot ever have enough recipes for a good chickpea salad. This one is mine, and I think it is quite divine. The creamy dressing has a sweet and tangy bite, which is mellowed out by the crunchy almonds and juicy grapes. This dish is equally amazing served on sliced bread or atop a bed of greens.

• • • • • • • • • • • • • • YIELD: 10 SERVINGS, ABOUT ½ CUP (112 G) EACH • • • • • • • • • • • • • •

3½ cups (800 g) cooked chickpeas (if canned, drained and rinsed)

1 tablespoon (2.5 g) rubbed sage

1½ teaspoons chicken-flavored vegetable seasoning powder, such as McKay's (optional)

¼ teaspoon salt

3 stalks celery, thinly sliced (about 1 cup, [100 g])

2 tablespoons (30 ml) lemon juice

½ cup (120 ml) vegan mayonnaise

1 tablespoon (15 g) spicy brown mustard

1 tablespoon (15 ml) agave nectar

¼ teaspoon celery salt

½ cup (60 g) sliced, toasted almonds

1 cup (150 g) quartered seedless grapes, any variety

In a food processor, combine the chickpeas, sage, veggie seasoning, and salt. Pulse briefly just until crumbly. Big pieces are totally fine, as are small . . . the size of the chickpea chunks will determine the texture of the salad. For a smoother salad, pulse the chickpeas longer.

Transfer to a bowl and stir in the celery, lemon juice, mayonnaise, brown mustard, agave, and celery salt until the salad is uniform in texture and color. Fold in the almonds and quartered grapes.

Serve on gluten-free bread or atop a bed of greens and devour!

RECIPE NOTE

To easily toast sliced almonds, preheat the oven to 400°F (200°C, or gas mark 6), spread the nuts in a single layer on a baking sheet, and bake for 5 minutes or until fragrant.

NUTRITIONAL ANALYSIS

PER SERVING: 320 CALORIES; 10 G FAT; 15 G PROTEIN; 47 G CARBOHYDRATE; 13 G DIETARY FIBER; 0 MG CHOLESTEROL.

STROGANOFF

Stroganoff was one of my faves as a youngster, even though I seemed to always avoid eating the beef tips. This recipe holds the same great flavor I remember, but it's animal-free!

• YIELD: 6 SERVINGS •

¼ cup (60 ml) olive oil, divided

I Vidalia onion, chopped

20 ounces (175 g) sliced cremini or button mushrooms

Salt to taste

I cup (235 ml) boiling water mixed with 2 beef-flavored bouillon cubes, or I cup (235 ml) concentrated vegetable broth

1¾ cups (420 ml) canned full-fat coconut milk, divided

I tablespoon (15 ml) wheat-free vegan Worcestershire sauce (or wheat-free tamari)

I to 3 tablespoons (8 to 24 g) sorghum flour, divided

I teaspoon black pepper, plus a dash or two

12 ounces (340 g) brown rice pasta spirals or flat, wide, white rice Asian-style noodles

Heat 1 tablespoon (15 ml) of the oil in a large skillet and add the onion and mushrooms. Cook over medium to high heat until the onions begin to brown and caramelize. Salt lightly. The mushrooms will produce a good deal of water as they cook. Continue cooking until almost all of the water has cooked out of them and the onions are translucent, about 10 minutes. Reduce the heat to low.

In a small heat-proof bowl, combine the boiling water and bouillon cubes, stirring to dissolve. Add to the mushrooms and onions. Add 1 cup (235 ml) of the coconut milk and let simmer for about 20 minutes, stirring occasionally.

Add the remaining ¾ cup (185 ml) coconut milk, Worcestershire sauce, 1 tablespoon (8 g) of the sorghum flour, and 1 teaspoon black pepper. Whisk together vigorously until very smooth, making sure there are no lumps of sorghum lingering in the sauce. Cook over medium-high heat, stirring continuously, until thickened, about 7 minutes. Whisk in some or all of the remaining 2 tablespoons (16 g) sorghum flour if needed to thicken even more. Add salt to taste.

Cook the noodles in a large pot of salted, boiling water for about 5 minutes or following the package directions. Drain and rinse briefly under cold water. Return the noodles to the pot and toss with the remaining 3 tablespoons (45 ml) olive oil, a dash or two more black pepper, and a touch of salt to taste.

Combine the mushroom sauce with the noodles while both are still hot. Top with freshly ground black pepper and serve.

NUTRITIONAL ANALYSIS

PER SERVING: 370 CALORIES; 23 G FAT; 8 G PROTEIN; 35 G CARBOHYDRATE; 1 G DIETARY FIBER; 0 MG CHOLESTEROL.

WALNUT RAVIOLI WITH VODKA SAUCE

Tender pillows of dough are stuffed with a meaty walnut filling and topped with a decadent vodka sauce. This meal is very hearty and takes a bit of prep work, so it's best reserved for a special occasion or an at-home date night.

•••••• YIELD: 5 SERVINGS, 3 RAVIOLI AND ¼ CUP (60 ML) VODKA SAUCE EACH ••••••••

FOR PASTA:

1 recipe Simple Homemade Pasta (page 22)

FOR FILLING:

2 cloves garlic, minced

2 cups (300 g) chopped walnuts

1 teaspoon minced fresh thyme

1 teaspoon dried sage

¾ teaspoon sea salt

1 teaspoon flaxseed meal

3 tablespoons (45 ml) olive oil

FOR SAUCE:

2 tablespoons (30 ml) olive oil

3 cloves garlic, minced

½ Vidalia onion, chopped

1 can (28 ounces, or 795 g) crushed tomatoes plus juice

1 cup (235 ml) vodka

1 tablespoon (15 ml) good-quality balsamic vinegar

2 teaspoons sugar

2 tablespoons (5 g) fresh chopped basil

½ cup (65 g) nutritional yeast

1 cup (235 ml) canned coconut milk

TO MAKE THE PASTA: Follow the recipe for making the pasta dough, but do not cook. Divide the dough in half and chill in the refrigerator while you prepare the filling.

TO MAKE THE FILLING: Combine the garlic, walnuts, thyme, sage, salt, and flaxseed in a food processor. Pulse until crumbly. Slowly drizzle in 1 tablespoon (15 ml) of the olive oil at a time and pulse to blend.

TO MAKE THE SAUCE: Heat the olive oil in a large skillet and sauté the garlic and onion over medium heat until golden brown. Reduce the heat to low and continue to cook until the onions are translucent. Stir in the tomatoes and juice, vodka, vinegar, sugar, basil, and yeast. Simmer for about 20 minutes or until you can no longer taste the vodka, stirring often. Remove from the heat and stir in the coconut milk. Set aside.

Roll out each section of pasta dough between 2 pieces of plastic wrap. You are aiming to make two 12 x 16-inch (30.5 x 40.5 cm) rectangles that are about 1⅛-inch (3 mm)-thick. In the meantime, bring a large pot of salted water to a boil.

Place about 2 teaspoons of filling evenly onto the dough, leaving a 1-inch (2.5 cm) radius around the filling mounds. You should have around 15 mounds evenly spaced on one layer of dough. Gently cover with the second piece of rolled-out dough. I use the plastic wrap to help flip one layer of dough evenly on top of the filling mounds. Use a pizza cutter or ravioli wheel to cut out individual ravioli. Seal the outside of the dough with a little water and crimp the edges with a fork so that the ravioli are watertight.

Boil a few ravioli at a time for exactly 2 minutes. Strain out with a slotted spoon and place in a bowl. Then add the cooked ravioli to the sauce and simmer for about 5 minutes. Serve hot.

NUTRITIONAL ANALYSIS

PER SERVING: 570 CALORIES; 32 G FAT; 18 G PROTEIN; 37 G CARBOHYDRATE; 10 G DIETARY FIBER; 0 MG CHOLESTEROL.

PIZZA FIRENZE

I like to think that my husband and I fell in love during art school in Florence, Italy. This pizza pretty much sums up our entire experience.

•••••••••••••••••••••• YIELD: 4 SERVINGS, 2 SLICES EACH ••••••••••••••••••••••

FOR PIZZA CRUST:

Cornmeal, for dusting

2½ teaspoons (7 g) active dry yeast

1 cup (235 ml) warm water

1 tablespoon (13 g) sugar

1 teaspoon salt

2 tablespoons (30 ml) olive oil

1 cup (130 g) sorghum flour

1¼ cups (198 g) brown rice flour, plus extra for rolling

½ cup (55 g) potato starch

1 teaspoon xanthan gum

FOR SAUCE AND TOPPINGS:

3 cloves garlic, crushed

1 cup (40 g) fresh basil

¼ cup (32 g) nutritional yeast

½ cup (75 g) walnuts or pecans

¼ teaspoon salt

1 tablespoon (15 ml) olive oil

3 tablespoons (45 ml) water

2 cups (200 g) nondairy cheese

1 cup (124 g) green beans, cooked

2 roma tomatoes, thinly sliced

¼ cup (7 g) minced fresh marjoram

1 teaspoon minced fresh thyme

¼ cup (40 g) small capers, drained

10 leaves fresh spinach, chopped

To make the crust: Preheat the oven to 400°F (200°C, or gas mark 6). Lightly oil a pizza pan or baking sheet and dust with cornmeal.

Stir the yeast into the warm water and sugar and let proof until foamy, 10 minutes. Add the salt and olive oil and stir to combine.

In a separate bowl, sift together the sorghum flour, brown rice flour, potato starch, and xanthan gum. Gradually add the flour mixture to the yeast mixture and knead until a stiff dough forms.

Turn out onto a parchment-paper covered surface. Lightly oil the rolling pin and roll the dough out into a circle ½- to ¼-inch (1.3 cm to 6 mm) thick. Fold up the edges of the circle to make a lip on the crust (if the dough begins to crack around the edges, brush on some water and rework a touch to smooth out).

Place the crust (using the help of a flat-edged spatula) onto the prepared pan. Let rest for about 10 minutes.

Place the pan on the center rack in the oven and bake for 15 minutes.

To make the sauce: Combine first 7 ingredients in a food processor or blender and pulse until a smooth paste forms. Add more water if needed, to make smooth.

Spread the sauce liberally on top of the prebaked crust. Sprinkle on the cheese and remaining topping ingredients. Lightly sprinkle on salt and drizzle with olive oil.

Increase the oven temperature to 450°F (230°C, or gas mark 8), return the pizza to the oven, and bake for 15 to 20 minutes or until all the cheese has melted.

Slice into 8 wedges and serve hot.

NUTRITIONAL ANALYSIS

PER SERVING: 450 CALORIES; 22 G FAT; 14 G PROTEIN; 54 G CARBOHYDRATE; 10 G DIETARY FIBER; 0 MG CHOLESTEROL.

SIMPLY SPECTACULAR TOMATO NOODLES

This is a fantastic recipe that my relatives have passed down for generations: pasta with not much adornment, but a whole lotta flavor. It's a tradition in my family to always add the hot peppers to the sauce, but I like it just as much without. If you're longing for a little more pizzazz in your pasta, though, try my all-time favorite variation: toss in some Cinnamon Roasted Cauliflower (page 141) along with the tomatoes and hot peppers and simmer. It's fantastic!

• YIELD: 4 SERVINGS •

16 ounces (453 g) brown rice pasta shells

3 tablespoons (45 g) nondairy margarine

1 very large Vidalia onion, chopped

Sea salt and freshly cracked black pepper to taste

1 can (28 ounces, or 784 g) whole tomatoes

¼ cup (34 g) jarred hot peppers (Hungarian wax or jalapeños), drained and minced (optional)

½ cup (120 ml) high-quality extra-virgin olive oil

Cook the pasta shells according to the package directions.

While the pasta is cooking or while you are waiting for the water to boil, heat the margarine in a skillet, add the onion, and sauté over medium-high heat until the onions are soft and translucent, about 10 minutes. Add about 2 teaspoons of salt to the onions while they are cooking. Reduce the heat to medium-low and continue to cook until caramelized, stirring occasionally, about 10 minutes longer.

Open your canned tomatoes and add one by one to the cooked onions, being sure to reserve the tomato juice in the can. Stir in the minced hot peppers. Once the tomatoes are in the pan, I like to cut them in half using a fork. This allows for the juices of the tomato to cook well with the onion. Let simmer for about 5 minutes or until hot.

When the pasta has finished cooking, drain well and rinse briefly under cold water. Return the pasta to the pot and stir in the olive oil. Gently salt to taste, if needed. I usually add about ½ teaspoon or so, but I like pretty salty food. Stir in the reserved tomato juice from the can. Add the cooked onions, peppers, and tomatoes and toss to combine. Cook over medium-low heat, stirring often, for 5 minutes longer or until hot. Top liberally with freshly cracked black pepper and serve hot.

NUTRITIONAL ANALYSIS

PER SERVING: 712 CALORIES; 38 G FAT; 8 G PROTEIN; 86 G CARBOHYDRATE; 4 G DIETARY FIBER; 0 MG CHOLESTEROL.

ROSEMARY, LEEK & POTATO PIE

My father used to make potatoes au gratin for dinner all the time when I was a little girl, as it was often just the two of us enjoying our meals together. This is a tribute to one of my dad's favorite dinners, with a few more "grown-up" flavors added in for good measure. Serve with a bowl of soup for a delicious, well-rounded meal.

• YIELD: 8 SERVINGS •

3 pounds (1.36 kg) thin-skinned potatoes, unpeeled and very thinly sliced (about ⅛ inch [3 mm] thick) into rounds

Sea salt

4 cloves garlic, minced, divided

2 tablespoons (5 g) minced fresh rosemary sprigs

1 leek, white and light green part only, cleaned well and thinly sliced

½ cup (65 g) nutritional yeast

7 tablespoons (100 g) nondairy margarine, melted

Preheat the oven to 400°F (200°C, or gas mark 6). Lightly grease an 8-inch (20.3 cm)-springform pan using margarine or nonstick spray.

Arrange the potatoes in one even layer so that they cover the bottom of the pan, overlapping as necessary with no gaps. Sprinkle lightly with sea salt, about one-fourth of the minced garlic, and a little fresh rosemary. Arrange a few rings of leeks (distributing evenly) on top of the potatoes.

Dust with nutritional yeast until all the potatoes are well covered and then drizzle with a little melted margarine (a little more than 1 tablespoon [14 g]).

Cover with a second thin layer of potatoes, then salt, garlic, and rosemary, and then a few more rings of leek, and finally nutritional yeast and a drizzle of margarine. Repeat the layering process again and again until all the ingredients have been used. Add a last layer of potatoes around the rim for an extra-special presentation. You should end up with 4 or 5 layers of potatoes.

Bake for about 1 hour and 5 minutes or until a butter knife easily slides through all layers of potatoes. If the potatoes begin to brown quickly, cover lightly with foil during the last 20 minutes of cooking.

Let cool briefly and then carefully remove the springform rim. Slice carefully into wedges and serve immediately.

NUTRITIONAL ANALYSIS

PER SERVING: 294 CALORIES; 11 G FAT; 9 G PROTEIN; 43 G CARBOHYDRATE; 7 G DIETARY FIBER; 0 MG CHOLESTEROL.

APRICOT RISOTTO

If you're intimidated about the process of making risotto, don't be.
It's really a cinch once you get the gist of it, and by the time all
the additions have been made, you are left with deliciously tender
and flavor-infused rice that is well worth the effort.

• YIELD: 4 SERVINGS •

1 onion, chopped

½ cup (65 g) chopped dried apricots

¼ cup (60 ml) olive oil

Dash of black pepper

1 cup (190 g) Arborio rice

**⅓ cup (80 ml) Chardonnay, warmed
slightly above room temperature**

**3 to 4 cups (705 to 940 ml) vegetable
broth, warmed**

⅓ cup (80 ml) nondairy milk, warmed

1 tablespoon (14 g) nondairy margarine

Salt to taste

RECIPE NOTE

For dishes like this, I enjoy cooking
with almond milk because it adds
a very subtle flavor and does not
curdle like soymilk tends to do.

In a large saucepan, sauté onion and apricots in the olive oil over
medium heat, just until the onions turn translucent. Add a dash
of black pepper. Remove from the pan using a slotted spoon and
place on a separate plate, leaving the oil in the pan.

Keeping the temperature at around medium heat, add the
rice to the pan and cook for about 7 minutes or until the rice is
golden brown, stirring occasionally. Add the wine and stir.

Reduce the heat slightly and let cook until all the wine has
evaporated or been absorbed. Add the onions and apricots back
into the pan and add a little vegetable broth. You just need enough
to cover the rice, about ½ cup (120 ml) to start with.

Let the rice simmer in the broth over medium heat until
almost all of the liquid has been absorbed. Stir often to prevent
sticking.

Add more broth and cook until there is just a little liquid left
to be absorbed. Keep repeating this process. It should take about
25 minutes of adding liquid in increments and stirring until the
rice is softened up. If you find that you are running out of liquid
too fast, reduce the heat and add less liquid at each interval.

Add more broth and keep cooking if the rice is still too firm
after 3 cups (705 ml) of broth have been added.

Once the rice is suitably cooked, stir in the nondairy milk and
continue cooking until most of the liquid has been absorbed. It
should look very creamy and the rice should be tender. Stir in the
margarine.

Cover with a tight-fitting lid, turn off the heat, and let rest for
about 10 minutes. Add salt to taste and serve.

NUTRITIONAL ANALYSIS

PER SERVING: 203 CALORIES; 18 G FAT; 6 G PROTEIN; 60 G CARBOHYDRATE; 1 G DIETARY FIBER; 0 MG CHOLESTEROL.

MAC 'N CABBAGE POLONAISE

This baked mac 'n cheese is a creamy rival to traditional baked mac and cheese with a little of my Polish roots thrown in. The cabbage adds a wonderful texture that is complemented perfectly by a crunchy crumble topping.

• YIELD: 8 SERVINGS •

FOR MAC 'N CHEESE:

1 package (16 ounces, or 455 g) brown rice elbow macaroni

7 tablespoons (100 g) nondairy margarine

¾ cup (97 g) sorghum flour

3 cups (705 ml) plain almond milk, divided

⅔ cup (86 g) nutritional yeast

½ teaspoon salt, or to taste

FOR CABBAGE:

1 head green cabbage, chopped into bite-size pieces

1 tablespoon (15 ml) olive oil

Black pepper

Salt

FOR TOPPING:

2 to 3 tablespoons (30 to 45 g) nondairy margarine

½ cup plus 2 tablespoons (81 g) sorghum flour

Dash of salt

2 cups (225 g) cheddar-style nondairy cheese, such as Daiya brand

TO MAKE THE MAC 'N CHEESE: Cook the pasta according to package directions and rinse under cold water. Drain.

In a saucepan, warm the margarine until melted. Stir in the sorghum flour until a thick roux forms.

Using a whisk, stir in about 2 cups (470 ml) of the almond milk and sprinkle in the nutritional yeast. Once smooth, allow to thicken just slightly over medium heat, and then whisk in the remaining 1 cup (235 ml) almond milk. Cook until thick, stirring constantly, about 7 minutes. The sauce should be quite thick and "plop" from the spoon into the pot. If you're having trouble getting the sauce to thicken, increase the heat slightly. Add salt to taste and combine with the pasta. Set aside.

TO MAKE THE CABBAGE: In a large bowl, combine the cabbage with the olive oil and lightly sprinkle with black pepper and salt. Transfer to a well-seasoned cast-iron or nonstick skillet. Cover and cook over medium heat until the cabbage becomes soft, stirring occasionally. Uncover and cook off any moisture if needed. If the cabbage still has excess moisture once it's cooked thoroughly, drain in a colander. Stir into the pasta.

TO MAKE THE TOPPING: In a bowl, cut the margarine into the sorghum flour with your hands or a pastry cutter until crumbly. It should be like small pebbles, rather than sand. Sprinkle in the salt.

Preheat the oven to 350°F (180°C, or gas mark 4) and lightly grease a 9 x 13-inch (23 x 33 cm) baking dish.

Spread a layer of the pasta and cabbage mixture on the bottom of the baking dish. Top with half of the cheese and then add another layer of pasta. Sprinkle with the remaining cheese.

Bake, uncovered, for about 20 minutes. At the very end, switch the oven to broil and let the top get crunchy (about 2 minutes).

Let cool briefly and serve.

NUTRITIONAL ANALYSIS

PER SERVING: 425 CALORIES; 20 G FAT; 11 G PROTEIN; 54 G CARBOHYDRATE; 8 G DIETARY FIBER; 0 MG CHOLESTEROL.

VEGGIES & DUMPLINGS

Chicken and dumplings was always my favorite comfort food—second to mashed potatoes, that is—especially during the winter months. This recipe utilizes my bizquix mix to make easy drop dumplings and it calls for a lot more veggies than the traditional version, giving it extra flavor and a fun burst of color.

•••••••••••••• YIELD: 10 SERVINGS, 2 DUMPLINGS EACH (PLUS VEGGIES) ••••••••••••••

8 cups (1.9 L) vegetable broth

1 large zucchini, chopped

5 medium carrots, peeled and sliced into rounds

1 Vidalia onion, chopped

3½ ounces (120 g) shiitake mushroom caps, chopped

3 ounces (100 g) cremini mushrooms, thinly sliced

4 stalks celery, sliced

1 tablespoon (2 g) dried sage

Salt to taste

1 cup (150 g) corn kernels, fresh or frozen

5 cups (625 g) Bizquix (page 25)

1½ cups (350 ml) nondairy milk

2 tablespoons (16 g) cornstarch mixed with ¼ cup (60 ml) cold water

Freshly ground black pepper

In a deep stockpot, bring the vegetable broth to a rolling boil. Add the zucchini, carrots, mushrooms, and celery and return the broth to a rolling boil. Reduce the heat to medium-low and simmer for about 20 minutes or until the veggies are tender.

Stir in the dried sage and add salt to taste, if needed. Stir in the corn and return the broth to a slow boil.

Next, while the broth is cooking, place the bizquix in a medium-size bowl. Gradually add the nondairy milk until a tacky dough forms. Use your hands to gently shape the dough into about 20 golf ball-size dumplings.

As you shape the dumplings, carefully drop them one at a time into the hot veggie broth. Once all the dumplings have been added, cover the pot and reduce the heat to medium. They don't all need to be submerged to cook; a few of the dumplings will inevitably end up underneath others. Cook for 10 minutes or until the dumplings are firm.

In a small cup or bowl, use a fork to mix together the cornstarch and cold water. Gently move aside a couple of dumplings from the top of the mixture and slowly add in the cornstarch slurry to thicken the broth. Let simmer until thickened, about 10 minutes, and then remove from the heat.

Serve warm (not piping hot or the dumplings will be soupy) and sprinkle with freshly ground black pepper.

NUTRITIONAL ANALYSIS

PER SERVING: 325 CALORIES; 10 G FAT; 10 G PROTEIN; 49 G CARBOHYDRATE; 4 G DIETARY FIBER; 0 MG CHOLESTEROL.

ASPARAGUS & MUSHROOM TACOS WITH CILANTRO MAYONNAISE

Taco night is always a favorite in our house, and we like to mix it up as often as possible. These feature asparagus and mushrooms and are an absolutely delicious way to spice up your evening meal. Try to find corn tortillas made from just corn, salt, and maybe a little lime juice, such as Trader Joe's brand.

• • • • • • • • • • • • • • • • • • • YIELD: 12 TACOS, OR 6 SERVINGS • • • • • • • • • • • • • • • • • •

FOR FILLING:

16 ounces (450 g) cremini mushrooms, thinly sliced

1 to 3 serrano chile peppers (depending on your heat level preference), stemmed, seeded, and minced

3 cloves garlic, minced

1 small onion, diced

2 teaspoons cumin

1 to 2 teaspoons red chile powder

¼ teaspoon chipotle chile powder

1 teaspoon minced fresh thyme leaves

1 teaspoon salt

2 tablespoons (30 ml) canola oil, divided

8 stalks asparagus, tough ends removed

FOR CILANTRO MAYONNAISE:

⅓ cup (5 g) finely chopped fresh cilantro

1 tablespoon (15 ml) lime juice

1 cup (225 g) vegan mayonnaise

FOR SERVING:

12 corn tortillas

½ cup (8 g) chopped fresh cilantro

1 cup (150 g) diced fresh tomatoes

TO MAKE THE FILLING: In a large frying pan, toss together the mushrooms, serrano chiles, garlic, onion, cumin, red chile powder, chipotle powder, thyme, salt, and 1½ tablespoons (22 ml) of the oil. Cover and cook over medium heat, stirring occasionally, until the mushrooms are tender and have released a good amount of liquid, about 10 minutes. Uncover and reduce the heat to low. Simmer until all the liquid is gone, approximately 7 minutes longer.

Slice the asparagus stalks in half down the length of the spear. Place in a separate frying pan with the remaining ½ tablespoon (8 ml) oil. Sauté over medium-high heat for 2 to 3 minutes or until bright green and tender. Set aside.

TO MAKE THE MAYONNAISE: Mix all the ingredients together until well combined.

TO SERVE: Using a flat skillet or cast-iron pan, warm the tortillas gently on each side until pliable and light golden brown. As each tortilla cooks, stack in a pile and cover with foil to retain heat and moisture.

Assemble the tacos by first adding the mushroom mixture, then the asparagus, then a little fresh cilantro, a few chopped tomatoes, and finally, the cilantro mayonnaise.

NUTRITIONAL ANALYSIS

PER SERVING: 172 CALORIES; 6 G FAT; 6 G PROTEIN; 26 G CARBOHYDRATE; 4 G DIETARY FIBER; 0 MG CHOLESTEROL.

BLACK BEAN, POTATO & CHEESE ENCHILADAS

The key to keeping the tortillas from splitting while rolling is to use the freshest and best-quality corn tortillas you can find. Generally they should just include corn, salt, and maybe a touch of lime juice. I always have luck locating these at Mexican groceries or even at Trader Joe's and recommend sourcing your tortillas there if you have one nearby.

•••••••••••••••••••••• YIELD: 12 ENCHILADAS, OR 6 SERVINGS ••••••••••••••••••••••

FOR ENCHILADA SAUCE:

1 cup (240 g) diced canned tomatoes, drained

1 can (8 ounces, or 225 g) tomato sauce

½ to 1 teaspoon sea salt

3 dried chile peppers (guajillos or chipotles)

2 cloves garlic, minced

1 tablespoon (7 g) cumin

1 tablespoon (15 ml) olive oil

2 cups (470 ml) vegetable broth

¼ cup (40 g) minced red onion

1 can (6 ounces, or 170 g) tomato paste

FOR ENCHILADAS:

2 cups (220 g) diced potatoes (dice small for faster cooking)

1 tablespoon (15 ml) olive oil

Dash or two of salt

12 corn tortillas

1 can (15 ounces, or 420 g) black beans, drained

2 cups (230 g) nondairy shredded cheese, such as Daiya brand pepper jack

TO MAKE THE SAUCE: Combine all the sauce ingredients in a saucepan and simmer over medium heat until the chile peppers are plump and rehydrated, about 20 minutes. Let cool and then process in a blender until very smooth.

TO MAKE THE ENCHILADAS: Over medium-high heat, sauté the potatoes in olive oil with the salt until lightly golden brown, stirring often to prevent sticking. Remove from the heat and let cool briefly.

Preheat the oven to 350°F (180°C, or gas mark 4) and lightly grease a 9 x 13-inch (23 x 33 cm) baking dish.

Pour about ½ cup (120 ml) of the enchilada sauce onto a large, rimmed plate or bowl. Have the rest of your ingredients, plus a large clean plate, lined up to assemble the enchiladas.

Dip one corn tortilla into the sauce, ensuring both front and back are completely covered with sauce. Transfer the single tortilla to a clean plate and fill with about 2 tablespoons (28 g) each of cooked potatoes, black beans, and cheese. Roll up to close and place in the baking dish seam side down. Repeat until all the tortillas are dipped, filled, and rolled, tucking each enchilada snugly into the baking dish. The proximity of the enchiladas should be enough to keep them from unrolling. Cover the enchiladas with the remaining sauce and sprinkle with any remaining cheese, if desired.

Bake, uncovered, for about 20 minutes or until the tortillas become slightly crispy on top. Serve hot.

NUTRITIONAL ANALYSIS

PER SERVING: 236 CALORIES; 6 G FAT; 8 G PROTEIN; 40 G CARBOHYDRATE; 6 G DIETARY FIBER; 0 MG CHOLESTEROL.

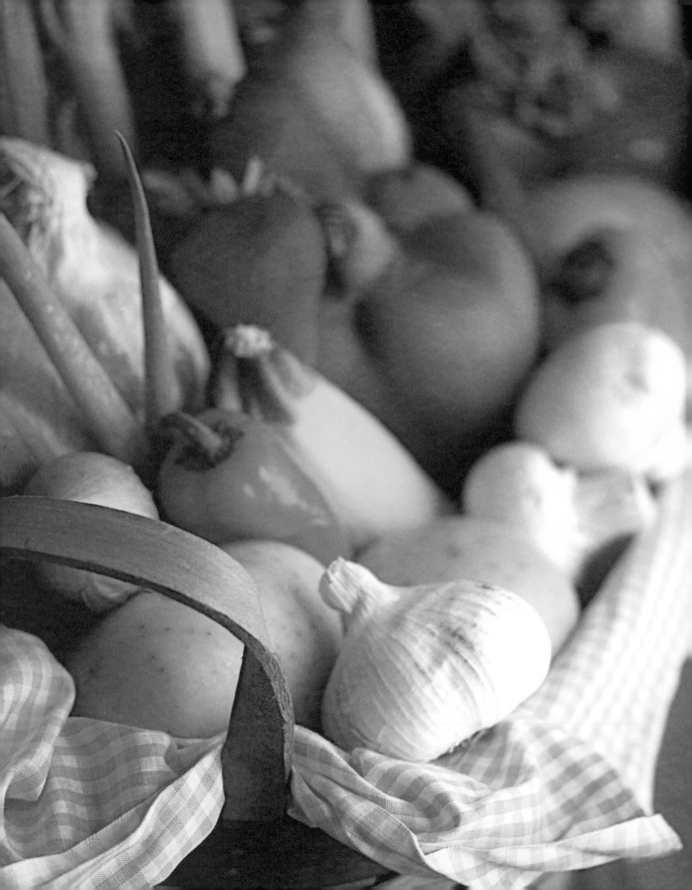

{ Chapter 4 }

SALADS & SOUPS

The following soup and salad recipes are ones where I had fun creating different and possibly unorthodox flavor combinations. A few of them are classics, though, and are the perfect accompaniment to many main courses in this book. The salads pair exceptionally well with the pasta dishes in this book. Try Greek Salad with Tahini Dressing (page 117) alongside a deep dish of Spicy Goulash (page 74) for an irresistible meal you will be craving over and over again.

QUINOA TABBOULEH

Instead of the traditional tabbouleh made with bulgur wheat, quinoa is used in this salad to make a gluten-free equivalent of the popular Lebanese dish.

• YIELD: 6 SERVINGS •

1 cup (175 g) quinoa, rinsed and drained

2 cups (470 ml) water

¼ cup (60 ml) high-quality extra-virgin olive oil

1½ teaspoons sea salt

2 cups (120 g) finely minced fresh parsley

½ cup (30 g) finely minced fresh mint

3 medium-size tomatoes, seeded and diced

Zest and juice of 1 large lemon

½ teaspoon black pepper

3 scallions, finely chopped

Combine the quinoa and water in a 2-quart (2 L) saucepan. Bring the water to a boil over high heat. Immediately reduce the heat to a simmer, stir gently, and cover. Let simmer for about 15 minutes or until all the water has been absorbed. Chill the quinoa in the fridge until cold, about 1 hour.

Stir in the olive oil and salt and then gently fold in the parsley, mint, tomatoes, lemon juice and zest, black pepper, and scallions until well combined. Let rest for at least 1 hour in the fridge until well chilled. Serve cold.

DON'T DO DRIED!

Fresh mint and parsley are essential when making tabbouleh. The intense flavors of these herbs just don't come through well in dried varieties and the fresh herbs add a nice texture and color to the salad.

NUTRITIONAL ANALYSIS

PER SERVING: 190 CALORIES; 10 G FAT; 5 G PROTEIN; 20 G CARBOHYDRATE; 4 G DIETARY FIBER; 0 MG CHOLESTEROL.

WENDI'S ZESTY BLACK-EYED PEA SALAD

This salad is named after my sister, who introduced me to this incredible concoction of flavors with a zing of Cajun spice tossed in. I consider this to be Wendi's signature dish, and it is, hands down, my favorite salad in the entire world.

•••••••••••••••• YIELD: 12 SERVINGS, ¾ CUP (170 G) EACH ••••••••••••••••

FOR SALAD:

2½ cups (375 g) cooked black-eyed peas

2 cups (330 g) cooked brown rice

2 cups (240 g) thinly sliced celery

1¾ cups (260 g) cooked sweet corn

1 cup (150 g) diced red bell pepper

½ cup (30 g) chopped cilantro

1 tablespoon (9 g) minced jalapeño
(remove seeds if you want less heat)

⅓ cup (33 g) chopped scallion

FOR DRESSING:

¼ cup (60 ml) apple cider vinegar

1 teaspoon cumin

1½ teaspoons Cajun seasoning

3 cloves garlic, minced

2 tablespoons (25 g) sugar or (30 ml)
agave nectar

1 teaspoon black pepper

⅓ cup (80 ml) olive oil

1½ teaspoons sea salt

TO MAKE THE SALAD: Combine all the salad ingredients in a large bowl and chill until cold, at least 1 hour.

TO MAKE THE DRESSING: In separate, smaller bowl, whisk together all the dressing ingredients.

Toss the salad with the dressing until well combined. Chill in the refrigerator for a few hours to let the flavors meld. Serve cold or at room temperature.

PLAN-AHEAD POTLUCK

This makes a great potluck dish because you can prepare the salad up to two days in advance and store in the fridge. The flavors have a long time to meld, and all you have to do is toss and serve.

NUTRITIONAL ANALYSIS

PER SERVING: 280 CALORIES; 7 G FAT; PROTEIN; 52 G CARBOHYDRATE; 10 G DIETARY FIBER; 0 MG CHOLESTEROL.

CREAMY POTATO SALAD

This recipe for potato salad emulates the same recipe that my mother still makes to this day. Mine has a few extra add-ins and no animal products, but the flavor and texture are exactly as I remember as a child.

•••••••••••••• YIELD: 10 SERVINGS, ABOUT 1 CUP (225 G) EACH ••••••••••••••

5 pounds (2.3 kg) Yukon gold potatoes, cut into 1-inch (2.5 cm) cubes

½ cup (120 ml) apple cider vinegar

5 tablespoons (70 ml) yellow mustard

2 cups (450 g) vegan mayonnaise

½ teaspoon sea salt

1 teaspoon celery salt

½ cup (75 g) minced red bell pepper

6 stalks celery, chopped to equal about 1 cup (150 g)

1 tablespoon (15 g) sweet relish

Paprika, to taste

Black pepper, to taste

Fill a large pot of water about halfway full with water, add 1 to 2 teaspoons sea salt and bring to a rolling boil. Carefully add the potatoes and return the water to a rolling boil. Begin timing your potatoes when the water has returned to a full boil. Cook for about 7 minutes or just until they can be pierced with a fork, but do not fall apart. These potatoes should not be cooked to the same consistency as you would cook mashed potatoes; you want them slightly less done than that.

Transfer the potatoes to a colander and drain well. While still in the colander, douse with vinegar, being sure to evenly cover. Place a plate under the colander and one on top to cover and place in the refrigerator until well chilled, about 2 hours.

Transfer the potatoes to a large mixing bowl and stir in the mustard, vegan mayonnaise, ½ teaspoon sea salt, celery salt, minced red bell pepper, celery, and relish. Stir well. If the potatoes seem to have held their shape too much, smash a few gently with a fork and then stir to once again incorporate the dressing.

Top with a good amount of paprika and fresh cracked black pepper. Serve very cold.

RECIPE NOTE

The cooking time on the potatoes is imperative to making the perfect potato salad. They should be easy to pierce with a fork, but not *so* fork-tender that they fall apart when stirred. A nice middle ground should be met, so that just a few potatoes break apart, creating a good base for the rest of the potatoes to swim in.

NUTRITIONAL ANALYSIS

PER SERVING: 415 CALORIES; 14 G FAT; 7 G PROTEIN; 66 G CARBOHYDRATE; 7 G DIETARY FIBER; 0 MG CHOLESTEROL.

SPICY EDAMAME COLESLAW

This coleslaw is slightly different than the typical American-style coleslaw because it features Asian-inspired flavors and coconut cream as the dressing base rather than mayo. It gets a little bit of a kick from the addition of Sriracha and just may become your new favorite coleslaw.

• YIELD: 8 SERVINGS •

FOR SLAW:

1 small head napa cabbage

2 cups (260 g) frozen edamame

FOR DRESSING:

1 ripe avocado, pitted and peeled

1 teaspoon freshly grated ginger

2 tablespoons (30 ml) mirin

3 tablespoons (45 ml) white miso

2 tablespoons (30 ml) rice vinegar

1 teaspoon wasabi powder, or to taste

4 heaping tablespoons (60 ml) full-fat coconut cream (the thickest part from a can of chilled, unstirred coconut milk)

¼ cup (60 ml) water

2 tablespoons (30 ml) agave nectar or (25 g) sugar

1 tablespoon (15 ml) spicy chili garlic sauce (such as Sriracha), or to taste

TO MAKE THE SLAW: Shred the cabbage and place in a large bowl.

Boil the edamame just until tender, about 5 minutes. Once done, rinse under cold water until no longer hot and drain well. Toss with the shredded cabbage and mix until the edamame is evenly distributed throughout.

TO MAKE THE DRESSING: In a bowl, use a fork to mash the avocado and then vigorously mix in the remaining ingredients until smooth. If needed, process in a blender or food processor; there should be no lumps in the dressing.

Toss the cabbage and edamame with the dressing until evenly coated. Serve immediately.

RECIPE NOTES

* You can leave the chili garlic sauce out of the initial mixing of the dressing and just drizzle on top to taste for each individual serving. This works especially well if you're sharing with little kiddos or folks who aren't down with hot and spicy.
* The best way to get the thick cream from a can of coconut cream is to chill the entire can in your fridge overnight. All the thick cream will rise and sit on top of the coconut water. Then you can simply scoop it out without worrying about separating. I have found that Whole Foods' brand of full-fat coconut milk works exceptionally well with this method.

NUTRITIONAL ANALYSIS

PER SERVING: 180 CALORIES; 10 G FAT; 10 G PROTEIN; 15 G CARBOHYDRATE; 6 G DIETARY FIBER; 0 MG CHOLESTEROL.

LATE SUMMER SALAD WITH CREAMY DILL DRESSING

This is a creamy twist on a summer salad I have been making since I was a child. I always got such joy from eating this salad in late July or August when our garden was abundant with vine-ripened tomatoes, fresh dill, and crisp cucumbers. Today, I still recommend sourcing ingredients from a local garden and eating in the shade of a tree while sprawled out on a blanket in the grass.

• YIELD: 8 SERVINGS •

4 or 5 medium-size tomatoes

1 or 2 medium-size cucumbers, peeled

3 tablespoons (45 ml) apple cider vinegar

1 block (15 ounces, or 420 g) silken tofu

1 or 2 cloves garlic (2 makes it extra tangy)

1 teaspoon salt, or to taste

5 tablespoons (20 g) chopped fresh dill, divided, plus several sprigs for garnish

Chop the tomatoes and cucumbers into bite-size pieces. Toss with the apple cider vinegar and let marinate for at least 30 minutes in the fridge.

In a food processor, combine the silken tofu, garlic, salt, and 2 tablespoons (8 g) of the fresh dill. Purée until very smooth.

Remove the cucumbers and tomatoes from the refrigerator, drain well, and toss with enough dressing to thoroughly coat. Depending on the size of your veggies, you may be left with a little extra dressing.

Stir in the remaining 3 tablespoons (12 g) fresh dill. Chill in the refrigerator until cold, about 1 hour, although this dish is wonderful if you let the flavors meld for a few hours before serving. Garnish with a fresh sprig of dill and serve cold.

KEEPING IT REAL

The original version of this salad can be easily made by omitting the garlic and tofu. Instead of draining the vinegar, let it remain as the base for the dressing. It is a bit lighter and a perfect snack for a hot summertime afternoon.

NUTRITIONAL ANALYSIS

PER SERVING: 43 CALORIES; 2 G FAT; PROTEIN; 2 G CARBOHYDRATE; 1 G DIETARY FIBER; 0 MG CHOLESTEROL.

EGGPLANT & CUCUMBER SALAD

Korean inspiration shines through in this salad with the combination of crispy cold cucumbers and warm tender eggplant. I took a cue from cucumber banchan, a favorite salad that I used to enjoy quite often during my college years, to create this unique dish. It makes an excellent accompaniment to Cold Sesame Noodles (page 69).

•   YIELD: 4 SERVINGS   •

FOR EGGPLANT MIX:

3 Japanese eggplants (about 1.3 pounds, or 600 g), peeled, halved, and cut into large bite-size pieces

¼ cup (25 g) chopped scallion

1 tablespoon (10 g) minced garlic

1 tablespoon (4 g) minced fresh oregano

2 tablespoons (30 ml) olive oil

¼ cup (60 ml) water

1 teaspoon salt

1 tablespoon (15 g) horseradish (freshly grated or jarred, not powdered)

FOR CUCUMBER MIX:

1 large English (or thin-skinned) cucumber, diced

2 tablespoons (8 g) chopped fresh oregano

Zest and juice of 1 lemon

1 teaspoon sea salt

2 tablespoons (30 ml) olive oil

1 tablespoon (15 ml) agave nectar

TO PREPARE THE EGGPLANT MIX: Combine the eggplant, scallion, garlic, oregano, and olive oil in a medium-size saucepan and cook over medium-high heat until soft, about 8 minutes.

Add the water, salt, and horseradish and cover with a tight-fitting lid. Reduce the heat to medium-low and cook about 10 minutes longer, stirring occasionally so that the eggplant doesn't stick to the pan. Remove from the heat and let cool to room temperature.

TO PREPARE THE CUCUMBER MIX: In a large bowl, combine the diced cucumber, oregano, lemon juice and zest, salt, olive oil, and agave. Cover and let rest in the refrigerator for about 20 minutes, allowing the eggplant to come to room temperature as you wait.

Drain the excess liquid from the cucumber mix and toss with the eggplant. Serve at room temperature or chill before serving.

NUTRITIONAL ANALYSIS

PER SERVING: 150 CALORIES; 10 G FAT; 3 G PROTEIN; 16 G CARBOHYDRATE; 9 G DIETARY FIBER; 0 MG CHOLESTEROL.

CARROT CELERIAC REMOULADE

This simple salad is an absolute favorite of mine. I find it to be the perfect accompaniment to the Mediterranean Croquettes (page 149), as the combination is simply divine.

•••••••••••••••••••••••••• **YIELD: 10 SERVINGS** ••••••••••••••••••••••••

4 medium-size carrots, peeled

1 medium-size celeriac (celery root)

2 tablespoons (8 g) finely minced fresh marjoram

Juice of 1 lemon

2 tablespoons (30 g) Dijon mustard

6 tablespoons (90 g) vegan mayonnaise

3 tablespoons (45 ml) olive oil

1 tablespoons (15 g) sweet relish

3 tablespoons (40 g) sugar or (45 ml) agave nectar

Using a grater or an attachment on your food processor, shred the carrots. You should have about 2 cups (220 g).

Remove the tough outer layer from the celeriac and shred completely (you may need to cut into pieces first if using a food processor). You should have about 3¼ cups (425 g). Toss the shredded veggies together in a large bowl.

In a medium-sized bowl, whisk together the remaining ingredients to make a smooth dressing. Gently toss the carrot and celeriac mixture with the dressing until evenly coated. Serve immediately.

NUTRITIONAL ANALYSIS

PER SERVING: 108 CALORIES; 8 G FAT; 0.5 G PROTEIN; 10 G CARBOHYDRATE; 1 G DIETARY FIBER; 0 MG CHOLESTEROL.

ORANGE, ARTICHOKE, ARUGULA & FENNEL SALAD

The various flavors and textures of this salad work so perfectly together that only a touch of dressing is needed to make a fantastic dish. I've always thought arugula to have an almost walnut-like flavor, which adds a nice earthy balance to the bright notes of the fennel and orange.

YIELD: 4 SERVINGS

2 tablespoons (30 ml) freshly squeezed lemon juice

1 tablespoon (15 ml) extra-virgin olive oil

1 tablespoon (15 ml) agave nectar

2 tablespoons (30 ml) freshly squeezed orange juice

1 teaspoon poppy seeds, plus a pinch for garnish

2 packed cups (58 g) baby arugula leaves

½ cup (100 g) thinly shaved fennel bulb, tough core removed (use a mandolin or a vegetable peeler)

8 small canned artichoke hearts, halved

2 medium-size seedless oranges, supremed (see Recipe Note)

In a medium-size bowl, whisk together the lemon juice, olive oil, agave, orange juice, and poppy seeds to make a thin dressing. Toss with the baby arugula leaves to evenly and lightly coat.

Gently stir in the shaved fennel, artichoke hearts, and oranges. Garnish with a pinch of poppy seeds and serve immediately.

RECIPE NOTE

To supreme an orange, cut off the top and bottom of the orange, so that the fruit sits flat on your cutting board and the interior of the orange is visible. Carefully cut the remaining peel off, following the curve of the fruit, until no more pith remains on the outside of the flesh. Over a bowl to catch the juice, cut along the membrane of each section with your knife from top to bottom and slice through to reveal each orange wedge. After cutting through the center of the membrane, the segments can easily be removed.

NUTRITIONAL ANALYSIS

PER SERVING: 98 CALORIES; 3 G FAT; 2 G PROTEIN; 16 G CARBOHYDRATE; 3 G DIETARY FIBER; 0 MG CHOLESTEROL.

GREEK SALAD WITH TAHINI DRESSING

Excellent!

When I first discovered Greek salad, my world turned upside down. I was smitten with the flavor combination and terribly disappointed at the idea of giving it up when going vegan. So I created this salad to replace my long-lost salad love, and man, does it ever hit the spot!

●   YIELD: 4 SERVINGS   ●

FOR DRESSING:

¾ cup (180 ml) extra-virgin olive oil

1 tablespoon (15 g) tahini

¼ cup (60 ml) lemon juice

½ teaspoon sea salt

1 tablespoon (4 g) finely minced fresh Greek oregano

2 tablespoons (5 g) finely minced fresh basil

½ teaspoon ground black pepper

1 tablespoon (15 ml) agave nectar or (12 g) sugar

3 cloves garlic, finely minced

FOR SALAD:

8 cups (440 g) chopped green leaf, romaine, or curly leaf lettuce

1 cup (100 g) pitted kalamata olives

1 cup (150 g) Tofu Feta (page 29)

⅓ cup (20 g) chopped fresh parsley

1 teaspoon lemon zest

Jarred pepperoncini (golden Greek peppers), sliced into rings, to taste

2 tomatoes, thinly sliced

TO MAKE THE DRESSING: Whisk together all the dressing ingredients until combined. Store in an airtight container and let rest for at least 1 hour. Stir before using. (If refrigerating, allow to come back to room temperature before using because it will separate when cold.)

TO MAKE THE SALAD: Shred the lettuce into bite-size pieces and toss with the dressing (use as little or as much as you'd like). Add the olives, tofu feta, parsley, lemon zest, pepperoncini rings, and tomatoes. Toss everything together gently before serving.

Divide among individual bowls and serve immediately.

NUTRITIONAL ANALYSIS

PER SERVING: 340 CALORIES; 33 G FAT; 5 G PROTEIN; 10 G CARBOHYDRATE; 3 G DIETARY FIBER; 0 MG CHOLESTEROL.

DRENCHED PAD THAI SALAD

Very Good make again.

This dish is similar to pad Thai, but made with raw zucchini "noodles." Even though there is no actual pasta in this salad, I find it hearty enough to serve as a meal because it contains grilled pineapple and tofu.

••••••••••••• YIELD: 6 SERVINGS, ABOUT 2 CUPS (240 G) EACH •••••••••••••

1 package (16 ounces, or 455 g) extra-firm tofu, well drained and pressed

For Tofu Marinade:

¾ cup (175 ml) pineapple juice

3 scallions, thinly sliced

2 cloves garlic, minced

3 tablespoons (45 ml) wheat-free tamari or soy sauce

1 teaspoon Chinese five-spice powder

1 teaspoon peanut oil or olive oil

1 can (15 ounces, or 420 g) pineapple slices in pineapple juice

2 or 3 zucchini

For Salad Dressing:

¾ cup (180 ml) liquid from tofu marinade

2 tablespoons (30 ml) lime juice

4 heaping tablespoons (64 g) smooth peanut butter

Wheat-free tamari or soy sauce to taste

For Salad:

1 mango, into bite-size pieces

½ cup (110 g) roasted peanuts, crushed

Chopped fresh cilantro (optional)

Favorite hot sauce (optional)

Slice the pressed tofu block in half, making two rectangles about ½-inch (1.3 cm) thick, and then cut into bite-size triangles. Arrange the tofu in single layer in a medium-size baking dish.

To make the marinade: Whisk all the tofu marinade ingredients together and then pour the marinade over the tofu. Let marinate for at least 2 hours, flipping the tofu halfway through.

Remove the tofu from the dish, reserving the leftover marinade.

To cook the tofu, place on an electric indoor grill (or mesh grill pan placed on an outdoor grill) and cook until golden brown on both sides, 10 to 15 minutes, flipping if necessary. While grilling your tofu, also grill the pineapple rings.

To make your zucchini noodles, remove the ends from the zucchini and peel if desired. Using a vegetable spiralizer or vegetable peeler, cut the zucchini into long noodlelike strips, chopping into shorter "noodles" if necessary, and place in a large bowl.

To make the dressing: Whisk together all the dressing ingredients until smooth. The dressing will be quite soupy. Add a touch more tamari to taste, if desired. Pour the dressing over the zucchini noodles and mix together until well coated, allowing the excess to remain at the bottom of the bowl.

To assemble the salad: Divide the drenched zucchini noodles among separate bowls, also transferring some dressing to each bowl. Top with the grilled tofu, mango, grilled pineapples, crushed peanuts, cilantro, and hot sauce. Serve.

Nutritional Analysis

Per serving: 430 calories; 25 g fat; 23 g protein; 35 g carbohydrate; 8 g dietary fiber; 0 mg cholesterol.

PUMPKIN CHICKPEA CHILI

Very Good make again.

I came up with this dish years ago during my yearly autumn obsession with pumpkins. It has become a simple dinner recipe that I enjoy serving just about any time of year, although we particularly enjoy it on brisk autumn nights.

● YIELD: 10 SERVINGS ● ● ● ● ● ● ● ● ● ● ● ● ● ● ● ● ● ● ●

1 onion, diced

2 cloves garlic, minced

½ green bell pepper, diced

½ to 1 teaspoon salt

1 tablespoon (15 ml) olive oil

1 cup (130 g) frozen or fresh corn

1 can (28 ounces, or 793 g) diced tomatoes

1 can (15 ounces 420 g) pumpkin purée

1 can (15 ounces, or 420 g) chickpeas, drained and rinsed

1 can (15 ounces, or 420 g) black beans, drained and rinsed

1 to 3 teaspoons chili powder, to taste

2 teaspoons cumin

1 cup (235 ml) vegetable broth

Zest and juice of 1 lime

Black pepper to taste

¼ to ½ cup (4 to 8 g) minced cilantro, for garnish

In a large skillet over medium heat, sauté the onion, garlic, green pepper, and salt in olive oil for 10 to 15 minutes or until tender. Stir in the remaining ingredients, increase the heat to high, and bring to a boil. Immediately reduce the heat to medium-low and simmer for 15 to 20 minutes until heated through. Garnish with fresh cilantro and serve hot.

RECIPE NOTE

Variations of this chili can be created by using different types of winter squash in place of pumpkin. Roasted and puréed acorn, butternut, or delicata varieties work well.

NUTRITIONAL ANALYSIS

PER SERVING: 277 CALORIES; 4 G FAT; 15 G PROTEIN; 48 G CARBOHYDRATE; 13 G DIETARY FIBER; 0 MG CHOLESTEROL.

SAFFRON-INFUSED WHITE CHILI

The white chili powder used in this recipe can be found in Indian groceries or can be easily substituted with another variety of chili powder to taste.

6 cremini or mushrooms, chopped

I Vidalia onion, diced

I yellow zucchini, unpeeled, diced

2 jalapeño chiles, stemmed, seeded, and minced (leave the seeds in if you like a lot of heat)

I yellow bell pepper, stemmed, seeded, and diced

I tablespoon (3 g) total minced fresh rosemary, sage, and oregano

4 cloves garlic, minced

2½ tablespoons (38 ml) olive oil, divided

Salt to taste

2 teaspoons cumin

I teaspoon white chili powder

4 cubes (4 teaspoons or 8 g) chicken-flavored vegetable bouillon

6 cups (1.4 L) water

I cup (100 g) textured vegetable protein (TVP)

2 cans (15 ounces, or 420 g each) Great Northern beans, drained and rinsed

I can (15 ounces, or 420 g) white kidney beans, drained and rinsed

2 tablespoons (30 ml) lime juice

3 tablespoons (24 g) cornstarch mixed with 6 tablespoons (90 ml) cold water

Small pinch of saffron threads, soaked in 3 tablespoons (45 ml) boiling water and allowed to rest for 2 to 3 hours

In a large stockpot, sauté the mushrooms, onion, zucchini, jalapeños, bell pepper, chopped herbs, and garlic in 2 tablespoons (30 ml) of the olive oil over medium-high heat until soft, about 13 minutes, stirring often to prevent sticking. Season lightly with salt, and then stir in the cumin and white chili powder as the vegetables are cooking.

In a pot, bring the bouillon cubes and water to a boil, whisking to make sure the bouillon is dissolved. Place the TVP in a bowl, add 1 cup (235 ml) of the boiling broth, and cover for 5 minutes, or until fluffy.

Once the veggies are soft, add the remaining 5 cups (1.2 L) broth and bring to a simmer over low heat.

In a small skillet over medium-high heat, sauté the rehydrated TVP in the remaining ½ tablespoon (8 ml) olive oil just until golden brown, about 5 minutes. Stir the cooked TVP into the veggies and broth.

Purée 1 can of Great Northern beans in a food processor until smooth. Stir the puréed beans into the veggies and broth until well incorporated. Stir in the remaining 2 cans of beans, lime juice, and cornstarch mixture. Cook for an additional 10 minutes over medium-high heat until thickened, stirring occasionally. Add salt to taste.

Crush the saffron threads with the back of a spoon and add to the chili. Let cook an additional minute or so before serving.

NUTRITIONAL ANALYSIS

PER SERVING: 534 CALORIES; 5 G FAT; 35 G PROTEIN; 90 G CARBOHYDRATE; 31 G DIETARY FIBER; 0 MG CHOLESTEROL.

COCONUT ASPARAGUS SOUP

Two of my favorite foods come together beautifully in this dish. The desiccated coconut adds a hint of texture to the puréed soup, and the asparagus incorporates a deep flavor and richness without the need for a cream base.

•   YIELD: 4 APPETIZER-SIZE SERVINGS   •

About 25 thin stalks asparagus, tough ends removed

1 small sweet onion, chopped (about 1 cup [160 g])

⅓ cup (30 g) desiccated coconut (unsweetened), soaked overnight and then drained

2 tablespoons (30 ml) extra-virgin olive oil, plus more for drizzling

⅔ cup (160 ml) water

Salt to taste

2 cups (470 ml) nondairy milk or vegetable broth

Steam the asparagus until tender, 5 to 7 minutes.

Meanwhile, combine the chopped onion, coconut, 2 tablespoons (30 ml) olive oil, and water in a shallow pan and cook over medium-high heat until the onion is tender and all the water has been absorbed, stirring often to prevent sticking, about 10 minutes. Lightly season with salt.

Chill both the steamed asparagus and the cooked onion just until cold enough to place in a blender, about 15 minutes. Chop the asparagus into bite-size pieces.

Transfer the veggies, reserving about ½ cup (50 g) of the asparagus for garnishing the soup, and the nondairy milk to a blender and blend until smooth, about 5 minutes. Add salt to taste.

Reheat on the stove top to the desired temperature. Garnish with a drizzle of olive oil and the reserved asparagus.

NUTRITIONAL ANALYSIS

PER SERVING: 106 CALORIES; 7 G FAT; 5 G PROTEIN; 6 G CARBOHYDRATE; 3 G DIETARY FIBER; 0 MG CHOLESTEROL.

SPICY KIMCHI SOUP

Because I grew up surrounded by a fairly large Korean community, kimchi was practically a staple in my life from a very young age. Kimchi soup was my equivalent to a hot bowl of chicken soup whenever I was feeling under the weather. Any ailment I had would quickly be knocked out by this spicy and incredibly tasty soup. I always serve this with a bowl of steamed rice to help cut the heat.

•   YIELD: 4 SERVINGS   •

3 cups (450 g) kimchi (your preference of spice level), undrained

2 scallions, chopped

1 stalk celery, sliced thinly

5 cups (1.2 L) vegetable broth

2 cubes (2 teaspoons) vegetable bouillon

1½ tablespoons (23 g) yellow or white miso

2 teaspoons wheat-free soy sauce or tamari

2 tablespoons (30 ml) unseasoned rice vinegar

2 teaspoons crushed red pepper flakes

Cooked rice, for serving

In a deep soup pot, combine the kimchi, scallions, and celery and cook over medium-high heat for about 10 minutes or until the kimchi is translucent and the other veggies are tender.

Add the broth and bring to a boil over high heat. Reduce the heat to low and stir in the vegetable bouillon, miso, soy sauce, vinegar, and red pepper flakes. Simmer for about 15 minutes until fragrant and heated through.

Serve with rice to help cut the spiciness.

RECIPE NOTE

Kimchi (also spelled gimchi, kimchee, or kim chee) is a traditional Korean dish made of napa cabbage and other veggies such as radishes, onions, or cucumbers. Because it usually contains red pepper flakes and is fermented, it reminds me of spicy sauerkraut. You can really taste the fermentation in a good batch of kimchi! It is a pretty easy thing to locate around the United States, but I've had the most luck scoring it at Asian grocery stores, where it's often locally made and you can buy a boatload of it for about one-fifth the cost at major grocery chains. Just be sure to check whether fish sauce is listed as an ingredient because sometimes it is used as a flavoring agent.

NUTRITIONAL ANALYSIS

PER SERVING WITHOUT RICE: 83 CALORIES; 0.5 G FAT; 5 G PROTEIN; 11 G CARBOHYDRATE; 5 G DIETARY FIBER; 0 MG CHOLESTEROL.

MINTED GREEN PEA BISQUE

This recipe is extremely easy to make and is always a welcome addition to almost any meal. Served hot or cold, it makes an equally perfect soup for a chilly winter night or a warm summer day.

• YIELD: 2 SERVINGS •

1 small sweet onion, minced

1 clove garlic, minced

2 tablespoons (30 ml) water

1 teaspoon sea salt, divided

3 cups (450 g) frozen or fresh green peas

2 tablespoons (12 g) minced fresh mint leaves

1 cup (235 ml) nondairy milk, plus more if needed

Fresh cracked black pepper to taste

In a small frying pan over medium-high heat, sauté the onion and garlic in the water until translucent. Season with ¼ teaspoon of the salt. Reduce the heat to medium-low and simmer until the onions are caramelized, about 10 minutes. Remove from the heat and let cool.

Bring a medium-size pot of water to a boil, and then add the peas and cook until tender, about 5 minutes if frozen or 2 to 3 minutes if fresh. Drain well and then rinse under cold water until the peas are cool to the touch.

Transfer the peas to a blender and add the sautéed onions and garlic, mint leaves, nondairy milk, and remaining ¾ teaspoon salt. Blend for 5 minutes or until super smooth. Add more nondairy milk if the soup seems too thick for your taste.

Warm gently over medium heat, sprinkle with fresh cracked black pepper, and serve.

NUTRITIONAL ANALYSIS

PER SERVING: 200 CALORIES; 1 G FAT; 13 G PROTEIN; 38 G CARBOHYDRATE; 13 G DIETARY FIBER; 0 MG CHOLESTEROL.

FAJITA SOUP

Excellent

My favorite part of this soup is the smokiness of the broth in contrast to the bright and colorful veggies. Topping with sliced avocados right before serving adds a little creaminess to this brothy vegetable soup. This soup is excellent served alongside a couple of Asparagus and Mushroom Tacos (page 94).

• YIELD: 6 SERVINGS •

½ cup (75 g) stemmed, seeded, and chopped red bell pepper

½ cup (75 g) stemmed, seeded, and chopped yellow bell pepper

½ cup (75 g) stemmed, seeded, and chopped orange bell pepper

2 cups (240 g) chopped zucchini

1 small red onion, thinly sliced

6 cremini or button mushrooms, sliced (about 1 cup [70 g])

2 tablespoons (30 ml) olive oil

1 can (15 ounces, or 420 g) black beans, drained and rinsed

1 can (28 ounces, or 794 g) diced tomatoes

6 cups (1410 ml) vegetable broth

2 teaspoons cumin

½ teaspoon chipotle chili powder

2 tablespoons (30 ml) fresh lime juice, plus extra for serving

Salt to taste

2 ripe avocados, chopped, for garnish

Heat a large frying pan over medium heat just until hot. Toss in the peppers, zucchini, onion, mushrooms, and oil and sauté over medium-high heat until the vegetables are tender, 10 to 15 minutes, stirring often to prevent sticking.

Transfer the cooked vegetables to a large soup pot and stir in the black beans, diced tomatoes, vegetable broth, cumin, chili powder, and 2 tablespoons (30 ml) lime juice. Add salt to taste. Simmer for about 15 minutes until heated through.

Garnish with the avocado and a squeeze of lime juice and serve.

NUTRITIONAL ANALYSIS

PER SERVING: 255 CALORIES; 12 G FAT; 13 G PROTEIN; 31 G CARBOHYDRATE; 10 G DIETARY FIBER; 0 MG CHOLESTEROL.

CHEESY BROCCOLI SOUP

The classic combination of broccoli and cheese is always a winner.
When made into a soup, it becomes some serious comfort in a bowl.

• YIELD: 8 SERVINGS •

1 Vidalia onion, chopped

2 cloves garlic, minced

1 tablespoon (15 ml) olive oil

¼ cup (30 g) millet flour

¼ cup (60 g) nondairy margarine

2 cups (470 g) nondairy milk

3 to 4 cups (705 to 940 ml) vegetable broth, or to desired consistency

1 recipe Cashew Cream (unsweetened) (page 30)

1½ cups (195 g) nutritional yeast

3 to 4 cups (210 to 280 g) broccoli florets, steamed until very tender and chopped into bite-size pieces

½ cup (45 g) nondairy shredded cheese, such as Daiya brand cheddar cheese (optional)

Salt and pepper to taste

In a skillet over medium-high heat, sauté the onion and garlic in olive oil until the onions are caramelized, about 13 minutes, stirring often to prevent sticking.

In a large soup pot, stir together the millet flour and margarine over medium heat until the margarine is melted and the mixture forms a roux. Quickly whisk in the nondairy milk and vegetable broth and stir continuously until smooth.

Add the cashew cream and nutritional yeast and continue to whisk to prevent lumps from forming. Stir in the steamed broccoli and sautéed onions and simmer for 5 to 7 minutes over medium heat until thickened. If the soup becomes too thick too quickly, reduce the heat and whisk in a little more vegetable broth to thin. Stir in the cheese and simmer over low heat until melted. Add salt to taste, if necessary.

Garnish with fresh cracked black pepper and serve hot.

NUTRITIONAL ANALYSIS

PER SERVING: 375 CALORIES; 20 G FAT; 23 G PROTEIN; 35 G CARBOHYDRATE; 10 G DIETARY FIBER; 0 MG CHOLESTEROL.

CORN & MUSHROOM CHOWDER

Creamy, hearty, and terribly addictive, this soup is terrific on a chilly evening with a crusty piece of Basic Brown Bread (page 26) while dreaming of fresh summertime corn on the cob. It's perfect if you've frozen some corn from the previous summer's bounty!

••••••••••••••••••••••••••• YIELD: 8 SERVINGS •••••••••••••••••••••••••••

8 ounces (227 g) cremini or button mushrooms, sliced

2 cloves garlic, minced

1 tablespoon (15 ml) olive oil

Salt to taste

1 small red onion, chopped (about ¾ cup [120 g])

3 large unpeeled yellow-skinned potatoes, diced (about 3½ cups [385 g])

3 carrots, peeled and shredded

8 cups (1.9 L) water

12 ounces (340 g) frozen or fresh corn

1 cup (235 ml) full-fat coconut milk

2 tablespoons (16 g) cornstarch mixed with ¼ cup (60 ml) cold water

Pepper to taste

In a skillet over medium-high to heat, sauté the mushrooms and garlic in the olive oil until soft, stirring often to prevent sticking. Season lightly with salt while they are cooking.

In a large stockpot, combine the sautéed mushrooms and garlic with the onion, potatoes, carrots, and water and bring to a boil over high heat. Reduce the heat to medium and cook until the potatoes are tender, about 20 minutes, stirring occasionally. Stir in the corn.

Reduce the heat to medium-low, stir in the coconut milk, add the cornstarch slurry, and simmer for about 10 minutes or until just slightly thickened. Increase the heat slightly if it is taking a while to thicken. Add salt and pepper to taste. Serve hot.

RECIPE NOTE

If a very thick soup is desired, double the amount of cornstarch slurry.

NUTRITIONAL ANALYSIS

PER SERVING: 188 CALORIES; 10 G FAT; 5 G PROTEIN; 25 G CARBOHYDRATE; 5 G DIETARY FIBER; 0 MG CHOLESTEROL.

VEGETABLE MISO SOUP

Kombu, an ingredient often called for in miso soup, is a type of sea vegetable that can easily be found in most Asian groceries and natural food stores. You can generally find it next to nori and other sea vegetables. This soup is similar to traditional miso soup with a generous amount of vegetables added in. Adjust the miso to taste. I like mine extra salty.

YIELD: 8 SERVINGS

4 heads baby bok choy, cleaned, ends removed, and roughly chopped

4 carrots, peeled and sliced

One 3- to 4-inch (7.5 to 10 cm) strip kombu (optional)

¼ cup (40 g) chopped scallion

1½ cups (225 g) chopped oyster mushrooms

½ cup (74 g) chopped enoki mushrooms

10 cups (2.4 L) water

2 teaspoons freshly grated ginger

1 teaspoon lemon zest

⅔ to 1 cup (165 to 250 g) miso (white, yellow, or red)

Lemon wedges, for garnish

Combine the bok choy, carrots, kombu, scallion, mushrooms, water, ginger, and lemon zest in a large pot and simmer over medium-high heat until the carrots are soft, about 15 minutes. Remove the kombu and discard.

Reduce the heat to low and stir in the miso, ensuring that all the paste dissolves into the soup. Simmer for a few minutes, making sure the broth never comes to a boil. If more miso is needed for saltiness, add it at this time.

Ladle into bowls and serve with a squeeze of lemon. Serve hot.

NUTRITIONAL ANALYSIS

PER SERVING: 30 CALORIES; 0.3 G FAT; 2 G PROTEIN; 6 G CARBOHYDRATE; 2 G DIETARY FIBER; 0 MG CHOLESTEROL.

APPETIZERS, SIDES & SNACKS

Whether you're in the mood for a light snack or a complementary side dish to a main course, this chapter has you covered. My personal favorite is the Pizza Crackers (page 153), which I have made again and again and again. For an over-the-top decadent dish, serve them with Spinach Artichoke Dip (page 158).

CINNAMON ROASTED CAULIFLOWER

This dish is my husband's absolute favorite. Its light cinnamon flavor and crunchy cornmeal exterior make for an elegant, easy, and unexpected side.

• YIELD: 8 SERVINGS •

1 medium-size head of cauliflower (about 2 pounds [910 g])

3 tablespoons (45 ml) olive oil, divided

3 tablespoons (27 g) cornmeal

1 teaspoon cinnamon

1 teaspoon sea salt, or to taste

Preheat the oven to 400°F (200°C, or gas mark 6).

Cut the cauliflower into bite-size pieces (about 1 inch [2.5 cm] across). Discard the tough core. Place the cauliflower florets in a large bowl and coat evenly with 2 tablespoons (30 ml) of the olive oil.

In a small bowl, sift together the cornmeal, cinnamon, and sea salt. Sprinkle evenly onto the cauliflower and toss with your hands until each floret is well coated. Add a touch more cornmeal if needed to evenly cover.

Transfer the cauliflower to an ungreased baking sheet (flat sides down), discarding any excess cornmeal. Drizzle lightly with the remaining 1 tablespoon (15 ml) olive oil.

Bake for about 40 minutes without flipping or until the cauliflower is crispy and browned on the edges and bottoms.

Gently remove transfer the cauliflower to a plate with a flat metal spatula. Serve immediately.

NUTRITIONAL ANALYSIS

PER SERVING: 113 CALORIES; 7 G FAT; PROTEIN; 11 G CARBOHYDRATE; 4 G DIETARY FIBER; 0 MG CHOLESTEROL.

LEMON ROASTED LEEKS

Lemon and leeks go hand in hand to make an incredibly easy and tangy dish to enjoy as a simple side or on top of Mashed Yukon Golds (page 33).

YIELD: 4 SERVINGS

4 large leeks

2 tablespoons (30 ml) extra-virgin olive oil

Zest and juice of 1 lemon (about ¼ cup [60 ml] juice, 1½ teaspoons zest)

¼ cup (60 ml) water

¾ teaspoon salt

Black pepper to taste

Preheat the oven to 375°F (190°C, or gas mark 5).

Remove the outermost layer of skin on each leek and cut off and discard the root ends. Slice the leeks in half lengthwise and clean well under cold running water. Be sure to open the leaves and wash out any grit or sand trapped in there. Cut at the point where the leek begins to turn green, and reserve the remaining darker green tops for soup stock. Arrange the leeks in a small baking dish so that they have room to lie flat.

In a small bowl, whisk together the olive oil, lemon zest, lemon juice, and water until well combined. Drizzle the dressing over the leeks. Season lightly and evenly with salt.

Roast for 35 to 45 minutes or until the top layer is crispy and browned on the edges and the inner layers are tender and easy to cut with a knife. The timing will depend on how large your leeks are.

Remove from the oven, cut into bite-size pieces, and serve with fresh cracked black pepper.

NUTRITIONAL ANALYSIS
PER SERVING: 114 CALORIES; 7 G FAT; 1 G PROTEIN; 13 G CARBOHYDRATE; 2 G DIETARY FIBER; 0 MG CHOLESTEROL.

BAKED CORN PUDDING

The easiest way to serve this classic dish, which is unlike sweet pudding and closer to a very wet cornbread, is by scooping it with a spoon, hence the name "corn pudding." I couldn't resist including this recipe because it has always been one of my favorite side dishes since I was a youngster.

•••••••••••••••••••••••••••• YIELD: 8 SERVINGS ••••••••••••••••••••••••••••

⅓ cup (80 ml) olive oil

½ cup (60 g) masa harina flour

¼ teaspoon sea salt

1 teaspoon baking powder

⅓ cup (47 g) finely ground cornmeal

¼ cup (60 ml) water

¼ cup (50 g) sugar

5 tablespoons (75 ml) canned coconut milk

2 cups (300 g) fresh or thawed frozen corn kernels

Preheat the oven to 325°F (170°C, or gas mark 3). Lightly grease an 8 x 8-inch (20 x 20 cm) glass baking dish.

Mix all the ingredients together in a large bowl until well combined. Spread into the prepared pan and bake for 50 to 55 minutes or until the edges are lightly golden brown.

Serve by scooping out with a spoon or small ice cream scoop. Best if eaten hot or slightly above room temperature.

RECIPE NOTE

Spice things up by adding finely minced jalapeños and some cumin, chili powder, and black pepper.

NUTRITIONAL ANALYSIS

PER SERVING: 184 CALORIES; 10 G FAT; 2 G PROTEIN; 24 G CARBOHYDRATE; 2 G DIETARY FIBER; 0 MG CHOLESTEROL.

COMPASSIONATE CALAMARI

This dish is deliciously crispy and reminiscent of actual calamari. But happily, no squid were harmed in the making of this terrific appetizer.

•••••••••••••••••••••••••• YIELD: 8 SERVINGS ••••••••••••••••••••••••••

Vegetable oil, for cooking

FOR COATING:

3 tablespoons (21 g) flaxseed meal mixed with 6 tablespoons (90 ml) warm water

¼ cup (60 ml) nondairy milk

¼ teaspoon sea salt

FOR DRY BATTER:

½ cup (30 g) brown rice flour

⅓ cup (47 g) ground yellow cornmeal

1 teaspoon dulse granules or flakes

FOR WET BATTER:

1 cup (140 g) finely ground yellow cornmeal

1½ cups (350 ml) nondairy milk

6 large king oyster mushrooms, tough bottoms removed, sliced into ¼- to ½-inch (6 mm to 1.3 cm)-wide strips

Sea salt, to taste

GARLIC TARTER SAUCE:

½ cup (120 ml) vegan mayonnaise

2 teaspoons sweet relish

1 teaspoon finely minced garlic

1 tablespoon (15 ml) lemon juice

Pour the oil to a depth of 5 inches (13 cm) into a deep fryer or deep pot and heat to 360°F (182°C).

TO MAKE THE DRY COATING: Mix all the coating ingredients together in a small bowl.

TO MAKE THE DRY BATTER: Sift together all the dry batter ingredients in a small bowl.

TO MAKE THE WET BATTER: In a medium-size bowl, whisk the cornmeal and nondairy milk together until a thick batter forms.

I find it easiest to have each mixture in a small dish in the order given so it's easy to dip the mushroom slices assembly style. Make sure your oil is at temperature before attempting to dip your mushrooms because it will be difficult to set them down once they are coated.

Dip one mushroom slice first into the coating, then into the dry batter, and finally into the wet batter, letting any excess drip off. The mushroom should be evenly coated. Drop immediately into the hot oil and quickly repeat with a few more mushrooms until you run out of room in your fryer. Fry for 6 minutes or until dark golden brown. Remove with a skimmer and transfer to a folded brown paper bag or paper towels to absorb any excess grease. Season lightly with salt, if desired. Repeat until each mushroom slice has been cooked. Serve immediately with the dipping sauce and enjoy!

•••••••••••••••••••••••••••••••••••••••

FOR GARLIC TARTER SAUCE: Stir together all the ingredients in a small bowl until thoroughly combined.

YIELD: 8 SERVINGS, 1 TABLESPOON (15 G) EACH

NUTRITIONAL ANALYSIS:

PER SERVING: 38 CALORIES; 4 G FAT; 2 G CARBOHYDRATE; 0 G PROTEIN; 0 G DIETARY FIBER; 0 G CHOLESTEROL.

NUTRITIONAL ANALYSIS

PER SERVING: 370 CALORIES; 30 G FAT; 3 G PROTEIN; 25 G CARBOHYDRATE; 3 G DIETARY FIBER; 0 MG CHOLESTEROL.

MEDITERRANEAN CROQUETTES

Reminiscent of baked falafel, this dish combines my favorite foods from
Mediterranean cuisine into crispy patties. They work well as an appetizer,
a main course, or even stuffed into your favorite gluten-free bread
and eaten as a sandwich. They are wonderful with a nice big dollop of Carrot
Celeriac Remoulade (page 112) on top of a bed of baby greens.

● ● ● ● ● ● ● ● ● ● ● ● ● ● ● ●   YIELD: 20 CROQUETTES, OR 10 SERVINGS   ● ● ● ● ● ● ● ● ● ● ● ● ● ● ●

4 medium-size Yukon gold potatoes,
   unpeeled, cubed into small pieces

4 to 6 cloves garlic, minced

1½ cups (350 ml) water

1 heaping tablespoon (15 g) tahini

½ teaspoon salt

1¼ cups (162 g) chickpea flour

½ cup (75 g) diced roasted red bell
   pepper

½ cup (50 g) chopped kalamata olives

⅔ cup (40 g) minced fresh parsley

1 teaspoon freshly cracked black pepper

Zest of 1 lemon

Olive oil for baking, or vegetable
   oil for frying

Combine the cubed potatoes, minced garlic, and water in a large
frying pan. Cover (with a slight vent) and cook over medium-
high heat, stirring occasionally, until all the water has been
absorbed or cooked away and the potatoes are fork-tender, about
15 minutes (you may need to add more water if the water cooks
off before the potatoes are done).

Transfer the potatoes to an electric mixing bowl and mix until
mashed or use a potato masher and mash by hand. Mash just
until well blended, leaving some lumps.

Stir the tahini and salt into the potatoes, mixing until just
combined. Next, stir in the chickpea flour until well mixed. Be
careful not to overstir. Fold in the roasted red pepper, kalamata
olives, chopped parsley, fresh cracked pepper, and lemon zest.
Chill the dough in the freezer for about 15 minutes.

Meanwhile, preheat the oven to 400°F (200°C, or gas mark 6).

Shape the dough into twenty 2-inch-wide x ¾-inch-thick
(5 x 2 cm) patties and transfer to a nonstick or lightly oiled
baking sheet. Brush both sides gently with olive oil and bake for
20 minutes. Flip and bake for 20 minutes longer or until golden
brown on both sides.

RECIPE NOTE

Biter beware! On the way to the freezer,
do not try to taste the dough . . . not
even the teensiest bite. Chickpea flour
has a very unappealing flavor to most
folks when eaten raw.

NUTRITIONAL ANALYSIS

PER SERVING: 203 CALORIES; 3 G FAT; 7 G PROTEIN; 32 G CARBOHYDRATE; 7 G DIETARY FIBER; 0 MG CHOLESTEROL.

STUFFED CHERRY TOMATOES

This is an irresistible finger food that's to be eaten hot from the oven. Well, not *too* hot because you'll burn your mouth; let 'em cool for a few minutes before offering them up for munching.

•••••••••••• YIELD: 13 APPETIZER-SIZE SERVINGS, 2 TOMATOES EACH ••••••••••••

1 cup (120 g) chopped walnuts

1 tablespoon (2.5 g) fresh sage

2 cloves garlic, minced

½ cup (75 g) chopped onion

1 tablespoon (15 g) apricot jam

1 teaspoon sea salt

26 cherry tomatoes

Olive oil, for drizzling

Preheat the oven to 350°F (180°C, or gas mark 4).

In a food processor, combine the walnuts, sage, garlic, onion, jam, and salt. Pulse several times until a paste is formed.

Slice the tops off of the cherry tomatoes. Using a small spoon, scoop out the seeds of each cherry tomato and discard the seedy filling. Fill each tomato with the walnut paste and replace the tomato cap. I like to overstuff mine so that the cap just barely sits on top of the filling. Arrange snugly in a small baking dish so the caps remain upright. Drizzle lightly with olive oil.

Bake for about 30 minutes. Let cool briefly and then serve immediately.

Tip

Prepare these appetizers ahead of time. For seamless serving, don't bake them until the guests arrive.

NUTRITIONAL ANALYSIS

PER SERVING: 108 CALORIES; 6 G FAT; 4 G PROTEIN; 12 G CARBOHYDRATE; 4 G DIETARY FIBER; 0 MG CHOLESTEROL.

PIZZA CRACKERS

I created these crackers to satisfy my late-night munchies, and every time I finish off a big batch, their addictive pizza flavor just leaves me craving more!

• • • • • • • • • • • • • YIELD: ABOUT 70 CRACKERS, 3 CRACKERS PER SERVING • • • • • • • • • • • • • •

2 cups (260 g) chickpea flour

½ cup (65 g) sorghum flour, plus more for rolling

½ cup (65 g) potato starch

½ cup (65 g) nutritional yeast

1 teaspoon xanthan gum

1 teaspoon sea salt

2 to 3 teaspoons ground pizza seasoning, plus more for sprinkling

⅓ cup (80 ml) olive oil

¼ cup (60 g) tomato paste

¾ cup (180 ml) cold water

RECIPE NOTE

I love pairing these crackers with my Quick Garlic Herb Dip (pictured). To make, simply blend together 1 cup (230 g) non-dairy cream cheese and ½ cup (115 g) non-dairy sour cream in a bowl. Stir in 2 teaspoons garlic powder, 2 tablespoons (15 g) chopped chives, 1 teaspoon each minced fresh basil and oregano, and ½ teaspoon lemon zest. Garnish with pizza seasoning and extra chopped chives.

Preheat the oven to 350°F (180°C, or gas mark 4).

In a large bowl, combine the chickpea flour, sorghum flour, potato starch, nutritional yeast, xanthan gum, salt, and pizza seasoning until well mixed.

Using a large spoon, stir in the olive oil, tomato paste, and cold water. Mix until very well combined. Turn the dough out onto a lightly floured surface and knead just until the dough is uniform in texture and color.

Add a little more flour to your rolling surface and pat out the dough to about 1 inch (2.5 cm) thick. Sprinkle the top with a touch more sorghum flour and flip over.

With a lightly floured rolling pin, roll out the dough until it is about ⅛-inch (3 mm) thick. Use a circular cookie cutter or a pizza wheel to cut out 1½-inch (3.8 cm) shapes of dough. Sprinkle with additional pizza seasoning.

Use a flat metal spatula to scoop up the shapes and place on an ungreased baking sheet, spacing them about 1 inch (2.5 cm) apart.

Bake for about 30 minutes, flipping once halfway through the cooking time. The crackers will have a reddish hue (from the tomato paste) but should be slightly puffy and golden brown on both sides when they are done. Depending on the size of your baking sheets and oven, you may need to make 2 or 3 batches of crackers.

Let cool completely. Stored in an airtight container, these will keep for up to a week.

NUTRITIONAL ANALYSIS

PER SERVING: 121 CALORIES; 5 G FAT; 6 G PROTEIN; 15 G CARBOHYDRATE; 5 G DIETARY FIBER; 0 MG CHOLESTEROL.

CUCUMBER PEANUT CHUTNEY

This is the perfect accompaniment to Potato Dosa (page 67) as well as a great appetizer to eat with chips or chopped veggies. You can find chaat masala at Indian markets or specialty spice stores. If you cannot locate it, feel free to substitute garam masala.

•••••••••••••• YIELD: 8 SERVINGS, ABOUT 3 TABLESPOONS (45 G) EACH ••••••••••••••

1 shallot, chopped

1 medium-size tomato, diced

1 medium-size cucumber, deseeded and chopped

½ cup (4 g) freshly chopped cilantro

1½ tablespoons (23 ml) lemon juice

2 tablespoons (30 ml) cooking oil

1 cup (150 g) raw peanuts

1 teaspoon black pepper

¼ teaspoon red chile powder

½ teaspoon chaat masala

Combine the shallot, tomato, cucumber, cilantro, and lemon juice in a food processor. Pulse briefly until well chopped but not puréed.

Heat the olive oil in a small pan over medium-high heat. Add the peanuts, black pepper, chile powder, and chaat masala and cook for about 2 minutes or until darkened. Stir occasionally so they do not burn.

Combine the peanuts with the rest of the chutney. Serve at room temperature or well chilled.

SERVING SUGGESTION: QUICK, SPICY TORTILLA CHIPS

Stack seven corn tortillas and cut into triangles. Arrange in a single layer on baking sheet; drizzle with olive oil. Sprinkle with garam marsala and salt and bake at 400°F (200°C, or gas mark 6) for 10 to 15 minutes or until crispy.

NUTRITIONAL ANALYSIS

PER SERVING: 140 CALORIES; 13 G FAT; 5 G PROTEIN; 5 G CARBOHYDRATE; 2 G DIETARY FIBER; 0 MG CHOLESTEROL.

BLUEBERRY AVOCADO SALSA

This fruity salsa is sure to delight as well as intrigue. It's best if made with fresh blueberries when in season, but frozen will work just fine.

•••••••••••••••••• YIELD: 3 SERVINGS, ¼ CUP (62 G) EACH ••••••••••••••••••••

2 large tomatoes, quartered

2 cups (290 g) fresh blueberries

2 tablespoons (30 ml) lime juice, plus extra for drizzling

¼ cup (40 g) chopped scallion

½ cup (8 g) chopped fresh cilantro

1 teaspoon sea salt, or more to taste

1 jalapeño pepper, stemmed, seeded, and chopped (leave the seeds in if you like more heat)

1 ripe avocado, peeled, pitted, and cut into small chunks

Combine the tomatoes, blueberries, 2 tablespoons (30 ml) lime juice, scallion, cilantro, salt, and jalapeño in a food processor and pulse a few times. Transfer to a bowl. Drizzle the remaining lime juice over the avocado chunks. Add to the salsa and stir to combine. Add a touch more salt if desired. Serve immediately.

RECIPE PAIRING IDEA

Use this as an accompaniment to the Asparagus and Mushroom Tacos (page 94) for an extra tasty meal.

This salsa should keep up to one week if stored properly in an airtight container.

NUTRITIONAL ANALYSIS

PER SERVING: 90 CALORIES; 5 G FAT; 2 G PROTEIN; 12 G CARBOHYDRATE; 4 G DIETARY FIBER; 0 MG CHOLESTEROL.

SPINACH ARTICHOKE DIP

As a frequenter of chain restaurants in my youth, I cannot imagine what my life would be like without the occasional decadent dish of spinach artichoke dip. This richly flavored dip is great for movie night when served along with your favorite tortilla chips.

• YIELD: 8 SERVINGS •

1 recipe unsweetened Cashew Cream (page 30)

½ cup (110 g) vegan mayonnaise

½ cup (65 g) nutritional yeast

3 cloves garlic, minced

2 cups (60 g) packed chopped spinach leaves

1 can (14 ounces, or 392 g) large artichoke hearts, chopped

3 scallions, sliced into small rings

1 teaspoon lemon zest

½ teaspoon ground black pepper

Salt to taste

Preheat the oven to 350°F (180°C, or gas mark 4).

Stir together the cashew cream, vegan mayonnaise, nutritional yeast, garlic, chopped spinach, chopped artichoke hearts, scallions, lemon zest, and black pepper until very well combined. Season with salt. Place in an oven-safe dish.

Bake for 25 minutes. Turn the oven to broil and cook for 2 to 3 minutes, or until the top becomes golden brown and crispy.

Serve hot with your favorite dipping chips or crackers.

TIP

If you are hosting a big get-together and plan on serving this dip, you better make a double batch—this stuff goes fast!

NUTRITIONAL ANALYSIS

PER SERVING: 296 CALORIES; 20 G FAT; 12 G PROTEIN; 23 G CARBOHYDRATE; 7 G DIETARY FIBER; 0 MG CHOLESTEROL.

{ Chapter 6 }

DESSERTS & BEVERAGES

There are few things in life I adore as
much as a good dessert and
a fun beverage to wash it down. In
this chapter, you will find many
of my favorite sweet treats
that are good to enjoy morning, noon,
or night!

PIÑA COLADA CUPCAKES

These cupcakes bring a taste of the Caribbean right to your very own kitchen with a pineapple cupcake base and an intensely flavorful coconut rum icing. Don't forget the cocktail umbrellas when serving.

• YIELD: 9 CUPCAKES, OR SERVINGS •

For Cupcakes:

¾ cup (180 g) nondairy margarine, melted

1 cup (200 g) sugar

½ cup (80 g) crushed pineapple, well drained

1 teaspoon baking powder

½ teaspoon salt

1 cup (130 g) sorghum flour

½ cup (65 g) cornstarch

1 teaspoon xanthan gum

¼ cup (60 ml) light rum

¼ cup (60 ml) nondairy milk

3 tablespoons (45 ml) apple cider vinegar

For Frosting:

½ cup (95 g) coconut oil, at room temperature (firm)

2 tablespoons (30 g) nondairy margarine

2¼ cups (270 g) confectioners' sugar, divided

2 tablespoons (30 ml) pineapple juice (from canned pineapple above)

1 teaspoon rum extract

2 teaspoons coconut extract

To make the cupcakes: Preheat the oven to 350°F (180°C, or gas mark 4) and grease or line 9 cups of a standard-size cupcake pan.

In a large bowl, combine the melted margarine, sugar, and crushed pineapple. In a separate bowl, combine the baking powder, salt, sorghum flour, cornstarch, and xanthan gum.

In a small bowl, combine the rum and nondairy milk.

Gradually add the flour mixture to the margarine mixture about ¼ cup (30 g) at a time. After each addition of flour, add a little nondairy milk/rum mixture. Repeat until all of the flour and liquid has been used. Mix vigorously until smooth. Add the vinegar 1 tablespoon (15 ml) at a time.

Divide the mixture among the cupcake liners and bake for 25 minutes or until a knife inserted into the middle comes out clean. Let cool completely on a wire rack before attempting to frost.

To make the frosting: In an electric mixer, combine the coconut oil, margarine, and 1 cup (120 g) of the confectioners' sugar and beat until smooth. Add 1 cup (120 g) more of the confectioners' sugar and then gradually add the pineapple juice, rum extract, and coconut extract and whip on the highest speed until fluffy. Add the remaining ¼ cup (30 g) confectioners' sugar and beat until stiff.

Using a pastry bag or a small plastic bag with a corner cut off, or with an offset spatula, pipe the frosting onto the cooled cupcakes and store in an airtight container in the refrigerator.

NUTRITIONAL ANALYSIS

PER SERVING: 462 CALORIES; 30 G FAT; 2 G PROTEIN; 44 G CARBOHYDRATE; 1 G DIETARY FIBER; 0 MG CHOLESTEROL.

CHOCOLATE HAZELNUT BROWNIE CHEESECAKE

This creamy dessert is frozen instead of baked and then thawed in the fridge to bring it to a cheesecake consistency. I recommend using an 8-inch (20.3 cm) springform pan for this. A bigger size can be used, but keep in mind that the smaller the pan, the taller your cheesecake.

•   YIELD: 12 SERVINGS   •

FOR CRUST:

1 cup (110 g) raw pecans
10 Medjool dates, pitted
½ cup (50 g) almond meal
½ cup (40 g) cocoa powder

FOR FILLING:

3 cups (330 g) raw cashews, soaked in water to cover for at least 2 hours, then drained
1 cup (235 ml) coconut oil, melted
1 cup (235 ml) water
¾ cup (180 ml) agave nectar or maple syrup
1 cup (240 g) nondairy chocolate hazelnut spread, store-bought (such as Justin's brand) or homemade (page 195), plus more for garnish
1 teaspoon vanilla extract

TO MAKE THE CRUST: In a food processor, combine the pecans and dates and pulse until uniform and crumbly. Transfer to a medium-size bowl. Add the almond meal and cocoa powder and stir to combine. Press the crust into the bottom of a springform pan.

TO MAKE THE FILLING: In a food processor, blend together the soaked cashews, coconut oil, and water until very smooth, about 5 minutes. Add a touch more water if needed to get the cashews to blend well. Stir in the agave, 1 cup (240 g) chocolate hazelnut butter, and vanilla extract. Spread the filling evenly on top of the crust.

Cover tightly with aluminum foil and place in the freezer for 7 hours or overnight. Let thaw in the refrigerator for a couple of hours before serving. Garnish with a drizzle of melted chocolate hazelnut butter. Serve cold.

NUTRITIONAL ANALYSIS

PER SERVING: 518 CALORIES; 43 G FAT; 8 G PROTEIN; 33 G CARBOHYDRATE; 4 G DIETARY FIBER; 0 MG CHOLESTEROL.

DARK CHOCOLATE CHIPOTLE CAKE

Spicy, sweet, and spongy, this dessert makes a nice alternative to plain ol' chocolate cake. Adjust the chipotle powder to your spiciness liking.

Yield: 10 servings

For Cake:

2 cups (400 g) sugar

1½ cups (350 g) nondairy margarine, melted

¾ cup (60 g) cocoa powder

1¼ cups (162 g) sorghum flour

½ cup (65 g) tapioca starch

½ cup (65 g) cornstarch

2 teaspoons xanthan gum

1 teaspoon salt

2 teaspoons baking powder

1½ teaspoons chipotle powder

1 cup (235 ml) nondairy milk

6 tablespoons (90 ml) apple cider vinegar

For Chocolate Glaze:

1 cup (120 g) confectioners' sugar

¼ cup (60 ml) nondairy milk

½ cup (40 g) cocoa powder

2 tablespoons (28 g) nondairy margarine, softened

To make the cake: Preheat the oven to 350°F (180°C, or gas mark 4). Grease a standard-size Bundt pan well and lightly dust with cocoa powder.

In a large mixing bowl, combine the sugar, melted margarine, and cocoa powder.

In a separate bowl, combine the sorghum flour, tapioca starch, cornstarch, xanthan gum, salt, baking powder, and chipotle powder.

Alternate between adding the flour mixture and the nondairy milk to the sugar mixture, scraping the sides as necessary. Once well mixed, stir in the vinegar 1 tablespoon (15 ml) at a time. Spread the cake batter evenly into the prepared pan.

Bake for 60 to 70 minutes or until a knife inserted near the middle comes out clean. Because Bundt cake pans vary, check after 55 minutes to make sure you don't end up with a burnt cake. Let cool completely on a wire rack.

To make the glaze: Mix all the ingredients together until super smooth. Make sure you wait until the cake is cool to make the glaze because it firms up quickly.

When your cake has thoroughly cooled, gently remove from the pan, place on a wire rack over a piece of waxed paper, and pour on the chocolate glaze. Let the glaze harden before transferring to a clean cake plate and slicing.

Nutritional Analysis

Per serving: 548 calories; 30 g fat; 4 g protein; 74 g carbohydrate; 4 g dietary fiber; 0 mg cholesterol.

PINEAPPLE CARROT CAKE

Not Good, too grainy tasting & icing was too sweet.

Carrot cake has always been one of my favorite special occasion cakes, especially with pineapple added. The pineapple provides an extra dose of moisture while not competing with the flavor and texture of the carrots. Now we celebrate with this animal- and gluten-free version that is just as scrumptious as the original!

••••••••••••••••••••••••• YIELD: 16 SERVINGS •••••••••••••••••••••••••

FOR DRY INGREDIENTS:

1¼ cups (162 g) sorghum flour

¾ cup (90 g) buckwheat flour

½ cup (65 g) potato starch

1 teaspoon xanthan gum

2 teaspoons baking soda

1 teaspoon baking powder

1 teaspoon sea salt

Dash of cardamom

1 teaspoon ground cinnamon

FOR WET INGREDIENTS:

1¾ cups (350 g) sugar

½ cup (112 g) nondairy margarine, melted

3 tablespoons (21 g) flaxseed meal mixed with 6 tablespoons (90 ml) warm water

1 teaspoon vanilla extract

2½ cups (375 g) peeled and shredded carrots

1 cup (165 g) crushed pineapple, drained

½ cup (75 g) applesauce

Preheat the oven to 350°F (180°C, or gas mark 4). Lightly grease and dust with sorghum flour two 9-inch (23 cm) cake pans or a 9 x 13-inch (23 x 33 cm) sheet cake pan.

TO PREPARE THE DRY INGREDIENTS: Combine all the dry ingredients in a large bowl and mix well.

TO PREPARE THE WET INGREDIENTS: In a separate bowl, mix together all the wet ingredients until smooth. Add the wet ingredients to dry and mix thoroughly until you have a fairly thick batter.

Spoon the batter evenly between the two cake pans and bake on the middle rack of the oven for 30 minutes or until a knife inserted into the middle comes out clean. If using a sheet cake pan, bake about 5 minutes longer or again until a knife inserted into the middle comes out clean. Keep a watchful eye on your cake toward the last 5 minutes or so to check for doneness.

Let the cakes cool in the pans for about 20 minutes, and then invert the cakes onto cooling racks. Let cool completely before frosting.

CREAM CHEESE FROSTING: Combine ½ cup (95 g) firm coconut oil, ½ cup (115 g) nondairy cream cheese, 4 to 5 cups (540 to 600 g) confectioners' sugar plus 2 tablespoons (30 ml) almond milk into a bowl and beat with electric mixer to make a quick and delicious frosting.

Not Good, grainy tasting cake & icing too sweet

NUTRITIONAL ANALYSIS

PER SERVING: 427 CALORIES; 14 G FAT; 2 G PROTEIN; 77 G CARBOHYDRATE; 2 G DIETARY FIBER; 0 MG CHOLESTEROL.

AVOCADO GELATO

This rich dessert may seem a little unorthodox, but trust me, the creaminess from the avocado makes one helluva frozen dessert. The texture of this gelato is great straight from the ice cream maker, but if you prefer a firmer consistency, store in an airtight flexible plastic container and chill in the freezer for at least 6 hours.

•••••••••••••• YIELD: 14 SERVINGS, ½ CUP (120 G) EACH ••••••••••••••

I can (13.5 ounces, or 378 ml) full-fat coconut milk

1¼ cups (250 g) sugar

3 ripe avocados

I teaspoon vanilla extract

1½ tablespoons (23 ml) lemon juice

½ teaspoon sea salt

In a small pan over medium heat, combine the coconut milk and sugar and heat just until the sugar has fully dissolved. Remove from the heat and pour into a bowl. Chill (I always toss mine in the freezer for a few minutes) until cold, about 25 minutes. Halve and pit the avocados.

In a food processor or blender, combine the avocados, coconut milk mixture, vanilla, lemon juice, and salt and blend until smooth.

Pour the mixture into an ice to cream maker and process according to the manufacturer's instructions.

CHOCOLATE-SWIRL AVOCADO GELATO

Just as the mixture reaches a firm state in the ice cream maker, drizzle a thin stream of about ½ cup (95 g) melted chocolate chips into the ice cream while the machine is running.

NUTRITIONAL ANALYSIS

PER SERVING: 201 CALORIES; 13 G FAT; 1.5 G PROTEIN; 23 G CARBOHYDRATE; 3.5 G DIETARY FIBER; 0 MG CHOLESTEROL.

DARK CHOCOLATE ORANGE CUSTARD

This is ridiculously easy, ridiculously rich, and oh so good.
This custard is dense and delicious and best reserved for an occasion when
your taste buds deserve a little something special.

• YIELD: 6 SERVINGS •

1 tablespoon (6 g) orange zest

1 teaspoon vanilla extract

1 bag (12 ounces, or 340 g) nondairy chocolate chips

1 can (13.5 ounces, or 378 ml) coconut milk

Mix together the orange zest, vanilla extract, and chocolate chips in large heat-safe bowl.

In a small pan, over medium heat, bring the coconut milk to a boil. Pour the hot coconut milk over the chocolate chips and whisk together vigorously but carefully until smooth and uniform.

Transfer to 6 single-serving dishes, cover, and chill in the fridge until firm, at least 3 hours. This is best served cold.

RECIPE NOTE

You can omit the orange zest and/or substitute vanilla extract with an equal amount of almond extract if you want to try different flavors.

NUTRITIONAL ANALYSIS

PER SERVING: 409 CALORIES; 29 G FAT; 4 G PROTEIN; 37 G CARBOHYDRATE; 3 G DIETARY FIBER; 0 MG CHOLESTEROL.

MANGO FRITTERS WITH COCONUT DIPPING SAUCE

You'll need a deep fryer for these or a skilled hand at deep-frying in a pot.
If that's not too big of a concern, make these as soon as you can.
You will not regret it.

• • • • • • • • • • • • • • • • YIELD: 6 SERVINGS, 2 FRITTERS EACH • • • • • • • • • • • • • • • •

For Fritters:

2 ripe mangoes

Vegetable oil, for frying

½ cup (88 g) yellow cornmeal

⅓ cup (42 g) plus ½ cup (65 g) potato starch, divided

½ cup (120 ml) almond milk

½ teaspoon sea salt

1 teaspoon ground cinnamon

Confectioners' sugar, for dusting

For Dipping Sauce:

½ cup (120 ml) crème de coco

1 tablespoon (15 ml) lime juice

Zest of 1 small lime

Recipe Note

Crème de coco is a mixture of coconut cream and sweetener used to make mixed drinks such as piña coladas. It can be found where mixed drinks fixings are sold. If you can't find it, use the thickest coconut cream you can find mixed with a little agave until sweetened.

To make the fritters: Peel and remove the pits from the mangoes. Slice the fruit into strips about 1 inch (2.5 cm) wide.

Pour the oil into a deep fryer to a depth of 5 inches (13 cm) and bring to 360°F (182°C).

Meanwhile, in a small bowl, whisk together the cornmeal, ⅓ cup (42 g) potato starch, almond milk, salt, and cinnamon to make a slightly thick batter. Spread the remaining ½ cup (65 g) potato starch on a plate.

Dredge each piece of mango in the potato starch and then immediately dip into the batter, covering completely. Hold over the bowl to allow extra batter to drip from the mango pieces. Be sure to dip each right before frying to make sure the batter goes into the fryer along with the mango.

Drop one by one into the hot oil and fry for 4 minutes or until golden brown. Remove from the hot oil with a skimmer and transfer to a paper bag or paper towels to drain. Repeat with the remaining fritters. Dust with the confectioners' sugar. Let cool.

To make the dipping sauce: Using an electric mixer or by hand, mix together the crème de coco, lime juice, and lime zest until fluffy.

Dip the fritters into the coconut sauce, take a bite, and fall back into complete mango ecstasy.

Nutritional Analysis

Per serving: 190 calories; 16 g fat; 1 g protein; 16 g carbohydrate; 2.5 g dietary fiber; 0 mg cholesterol.

CHERRY-APRICOT POCKET PIES

These flaky little pocket pies are the perfect treat to whip up
when you're craving a fruit-filled pastry, but pulling together
an entire pie seems overwhelming.

••••••••••••••••••••• YIELD: 6 POCKET PIES, OR 12 SERVINGS •••••••••••••••••••••

FOR FILLING:

2 cups (470 ml) water

⅓ cup (50 g) dried cherries

1 cup (150 g) chopped dried apricots

¼ cup (50 g) plus 2 tablespoons (25 g) sugar, divided

1½ tablespoons (12 g) cornstarch

2 teaspoons flaxseed meal

Dash of salt

¼ teaspoon ground cinnamon

1 recipe Easygoing Pie Crust (page 34), chilled for at least 2 hours

RECIPE NOTES
* If fresh apricots and cherries are available, use those (pit and dice the fruit) and skip the boiling step.
* To make a glaze, whisk ½ cup (60 g) confectioners' sugar with 2 tablespoons (30 ml) nondairy milk until smooth. Stir in a teaspoon or so of corn syrup or agave nectar to make shiny, and flavor with a drop of your favorite extract.

Preheat the oven to 375°F (190°C, or gas mark 5).

TO MAKE THE FILLING: Pour the water into a medium-size saucepan and bring to a boil over high heat. Add the dried fruits, reduce the heat to medium, and cook until the apricots are very soft but not mushy, 5 to 7 minutes. Drain the fruit and set aside to cool.

Add the ¼ cup (50 g) sugar, cornstarch, flaxseed, salt, and cinnamon to the fruit and stir to combine.

Place the chilled pie crust dough between 2 large pieces of parchment paper and roll out to ¼ inch (6 mm) thick. Use a large biscuit cutter or a small bowl (about 5 inches [13 cm] wide) turned upside down to cut out 6 circles of dough, gathering up the dough and rerolling as necessary.

Place about 2 tablespoons (30 g) of the filling onto half of each circle crust, leaving about a ½-inch (1.3 cm) edge around the filling. Fold the dough over the fruit filling, pressing together the edges to seal. Crimp the edges with a fork and cut a few slits in the top of the crust. The dough will be slightly fragile, so handle with care. Sprinkle with the remaining 2 tablespoons (28 g) sugar and place on an ungreased baking sheet.

Bake for about 28 minutes or until lightly golden brown on the edges. Let cool. Drizzle with glaze, if desired (see Recipe Notes).

NUTRITIONAL ANALYSIS

PER SERVING: 310 CALORIES; 17 G FAT; 2 G PROTEIN; 38 G CARBOHYDRATE; 2 G DIETARY FIBER; 0 MG CHOLESTEROL.

COCONUT RICE WITH PEACHES & RUM RAISINS

This recipe is a more exotic take on the average rice pudding with its extra-creamy texture and sweet and tart flavors of fruit laced throughout. For a non-boozy option, soak the raisins in ½ cup (120 ml) pineapple juice mixed with 2 teaspoons rum extract.

• YIELD: 8 SERVINGS •

½ cup (120 ml) light rum

1 cup (145 g) raisins

2 cups (390 g) uncooked jasmine rice

4 cups (940 ml) water

1 can (13.5 ounces, or 378 ml) coconut milk

1 cup (200 g) sugar

Dash of salt to taste (optional)

2 or 3 ripe peaches, chopped

Ground cinnamon, for sprinkling

The night before, combine the rum and raisins in a small bowl and cover. Let rest in the fridge overnight.

In a 1½-quart (1.4 L) saucepan over medium-high heat, add the rice, water, and coconut milk, stirring to combine. Bring the rice just to the beginning of a boil (not rolling) and then reduce the heat to low. Cover and let simmer until all the liquid has been absorbed and the rice is fluffy, 20 to 25 minutes. Do not stir the rice while it is cooking and avoid lifting the lid more than absolutely necessary.

Once the rice is fully cooked, stir in the sugar. Season lightly with salt.

In a small saucepan, stir together the peaches and rum raisins (including the liquid) and cook over medium heat, stirring occasionally, until the peaches are soft, about 2 minutes. Drain and gently stir the fruit into the rice.

Sprinkle with a touch of cinnamon. Serve hot or cold.

NUTRITIONAL ANALYSIS

PER SERVING: 463 CALORIES; 12 G FAT; 5 G PROTEIN; 80 G CARBOHYDRATE; 4 G DIETARY FIBER; 0 MG CHOLESTEROL.

BANANA BERRY COBBLER

Bananas add an unconventional spin on a timeless classic with this fruity cobbler. This texture of this dessert is similar to a coffeecake on the top but with a tantalizingly sweet baked fruit layer on the bottom.

Yield: 12 servings

½ cup (112 g) plus 2 tablespoons (28 g) nondairy margarine, divided

1 cup (130 g) sorghum flour

½ cup (79 g) brown rice flour

½ cup (65 g) tapioca starch

1 teaspoon xanthan gum

1 tablespoon (15 g) baking powder

1 teaspoon sea salt

¼ cup plus 2 tablespoons (90 g) packed brown sugar, divided

1 cup (235 ml) nondairy milk

1 teaspoon vanilla extract

3 or 4 bananas, sliced

2 cups (290 g) blueberries, raspberries, and/or blackberries

3 tablespoons (38 g) granulated sugar

2 teaspoons lemon juice

Preheat the oven to 350°F (180°C, or gas mark 4). Place the 2 tablespoons (28 g) margarine in an 11 x 7-inch (28 x 18 cm) baking dish. Place in the oven until the margarine melts. Remove the pan from the oven, tip to coat the bottom, and set aside.

In a large bowl, combine the sorghum flour, brown rice flour, tapioca starch, xanthan gum, baking powder, and salt. Using 2 butter knives or a pastry cutter, cut in the remaining ½ cup (112 g) margarine until small crumb form. Stir in the ¼ cup (60 g) brown sugar until well mixed. Add the nondairy milk and vanilla extract, stirring until a thick batter forms.

In a separate bowl, toss together the sliced bananas and berries with the granulated sugar and lemon juice. Spoon the fruit into the baking dish over the melted margarine.

Drop the batter by the spoonful over the bananas and berries to mostly cover the fruit. Sprinkle with the remaining 2 tablespoons (30 g) brown sugar and bake for 45 minutes or until the fruit is bubbly and the top is golden brown. Let cool for about 15 minutes before serving.

Nutritional Analysis

Per serving: 217 calories; 9 g fat; 2 g protein; 34 g carbohydrate; 3 g dietary fiber; 0 mg cholesterol.

CHOCOLATE MARZIPAN TART

My family seems to think that this tastes like a brownie pie, but the almond flavor shines through delicately, making it undeniably all about the marzipan.

YIELD: 8 SERVINGS

1 recipe Easygoing Pie Crust (page 34)

FOR FILLING:

¾ cup (97 g) sorghum flour

¼ cup (32 g) tapioca starch

1 teaspoon baking powder

⅛ teaspoon salt

2 tablespoons (28 g) nondairy margarine

8 ounces (227 g) nondairy almond paste or marzipan

⅓ cup (65 g) sugar

1 tablespoon (15 ml) vanilla extract

2 tablespoons (14 g) flaxseed meal mixed with ¼ cup (60 ml) warm water

¼ cup (60 ml) almond milk

1 cup (175 g) nondairy chocolate chips

Preheat the oven to 350°F (180°C, or gas mark 4). Lightly grease an 8-inch (20 cm) tart pan.

On a floured surface, roll out the pie crust until about ¼-inch (6 mm) thick and about 14 inches (36 cm) in diameter. I find it easy to do this on silicone mats because you can easily move the rolled-out dough and flip it into the tart pan. Transfer the dough to the prepared pan and press into the pan. Trim off the excess dough. Place the crust in the fridge while you prepare the filling.

TO MAKE THE FILLING: Combine the sorghum flour, tapioca starch, baking powder, salt, margarine, almond paste, sugar, vanilla, prepared flaxseed mixture, and almond milk in a food processor and blend until smooth.

In a microwave or over double boiler, melt the chocolate chips and stir until smooth. Add to the food processor and process until blended. Spread the filling into the crust evenly.

Bake for 30 minutes or until the crust is light golden brown around the edges and the filling puffs up and begins to crack, similar to what a brownie looks like when done.

NUTRITIONAL ANALYSIS

PER SERVING: 408 CALORIES; 18 G FAT; 4 G PROTEIN; 60 G CARBOHYDRATE; 2 G DIETARY FIBER; 0 MG CHOLESTEROL.

SOULHAUS COOKIES

excellent

These chewy chocolate chippers are a delicious excuse to heat up your oven, and they will inevitably have a warming effect on your soul. Inspired by the classic Nestlé Tollhouse Cookie, these cookies alone make gluten-free vegan baking so very worth the extra flours required.

· YIELD: 24 COOKIES, OR SERVINGS ·

1 cup (225 g) nondairy margarine
¾ cup (170 g) packed brown sugar
¾ cup (150 g) granulated sugar
1 teaspoon sea salt
1 teaspoon baking soda
2 teaspoons vanilla extract
2 tablespoons (21 g) flaxseed meal
  mixed with ¼ cup (60 ml) warm water
1½ cups (195 g) sorghum flour
1 cup (158 g) brown rice flour
½ cup (65 g) tapioca starch
1 teaspoon xanthan gum
1 cup (175 g) nondairy chocolate chips

Preheat the oven to 375°F (190°C, or gas mark 5).

In an electric mixer, cream together the margarine, sugars, salt, baking soda, and vanilla extract. Stir in the prepared flaxseed meal.

In a separate, smaller bowl, combine the sorghum flour, brown rice flour, tapioca starch, and xanthan gum.

On low speed, gradually add the flour mixture to the sugar mixture until well combined. At first, your dough will be crumbly. Keep mixing (you may need to increase your speed a touch) until you achieve a soft cookie dough. Fold in the chocolate chips. Chill the dough briefly in the freezer until cold.

Scoop about 1 tablespoon (15 g) of dough onto an ungreased baking sheet, leaving about 2 inches (2.5 cm) between each cookie.

Bake for 11 minutes and immediately remove from the oven. The cookies will not look done at this point, but trust me, they are.

Depending on the size of your baking sheet, you may need to make three separate batches. Chill extra dough in the fridge while waiting to bake.

Allow the baked cookies to remain on the baking sheet until completely cool. This could take up to 1 hour. Basically, when the chocolate chips have returned to a firm state, they are ready to eat. If you try to move them too soon, they will most definitely fall apart, so let them cool!

NUTRITIONAL ANALYSIS

PER SERVING: 231 CALORIES; 11 G FAT; 1 G PROTEIN; 32 G CARBOHYDRATE; 2 G DIETARY FIBER; 0 MG CHOLESTEROL.

LEMON BISCOTTI

This biscotti has a light lemony flavor, making it the perfect accompaniment to a hot mug of tea. These biscotti are somewhat softer than those found at your local coffeehouse; bake about 1 or 2 minutes longer than recommended on each side if you'd like an extra-crunchy cookie.

• YIELD: 24 BISCOTTI, OR SERVINGS • • • • • • • • • • • • • • • • • • •

1 cup (200 g) sugar

½ cup (120 ml) olive oil

3 tablespoons (45 ml) lemon juice

1 teaspoon vanilla extract

1 teaspoon lemon zest

3 tablespoons (45 ml) nondairy milk

3 tablespoons (21 g) flaxseed meal mixed with 6 tablespoons (90 ml) warm water

1½ cups (195 g) sorghum flour

¾ cup (96 g) brown rice flour

¾ cup (96 g) potato starch

¼ cup (32 g) tapioca starch

1 teaspoon xanthan gum

1 teaspoon sea salt

1 tablespoon (15 g) baking powder

Preheat the oven to 375°F (190°C, or gas mark 5).

In a large mixing bowl, stir together the sugar, olive oil, lemon juice, vanilla extract, lemon zest, nondairy milk, and prepared flaxseed meal.

In a separate bowl, sift together the sorghum flour, brown rice flour, potato starch, tapioca starch, xanthan gum, sea salt, and baking powder. Gradually add the flour mixture to the sugar mixture and combine until a stiff dough forms. If mixing by hand, you'll have to knead it a bit to get it smooth. The dough will be slightly tacky when handling.

Divide the dough in half and shape into 2 long ovals, each about 3½ inches (9 cm)-wide, 9 inches (23 cm)-long, and ¾ inch (2 cm) tall. I found it easiest to shape them directly on my parchment- or silicone-mat-lined baking sheets using slightly wet hands.

Bake for 25 minutes and then remove from the oven and let cool, at least 20 minutes.

Once cooled, slice across the dough diagonally, cutting each log into approximately twelve ¾-inch-wide x 4½-inch-long (2 x 11.5 cm) cookies, varying slightly in length. Place each cookie on its side and bake for an additional 9 minutes. Flip over and bake the other side for 9 to 11 minutes or until golden brown on the edges.

Let cool completely before serving. These are best served a few hours after cooling.

NUTRITIONAL ANALYSIS

PER SERVING: 138 CALORIES; 5 G FAT; 1 G PROTEIN; 21 G CARBOHYDRATE; 1 G DIETARY FIBER; 0 MG CHOLESTEROL.

PEANUT BUTTER COOKIES

Excellent

Naturally flourless, these cookies pack in a whole lotta peanutty flavor and have a soft texture to boot! Be sure to let them cool completely before trying to pick them up, or they'll most definitely crumble.

• YIELD: 20 COOKIES, OR 10 SERVINGS • • • • • • • • • • • • • • • • •

- **2 cups (500 g) smooth natural peanut butter**
- **1¾ cups (350 g) sugar, plus extra for sprinkling**
- **1 teaspoon salt**
- **2 teaspoons baking soda**
- **2 teaspoons vanilla extract**
- **2 tablespoons (15 g) flaxseed meal mixed with ¼ cup (60 ml) warm water**

Preheat the oven to 350°F (180°C, or gas mark 4).

Mix together the peanut butter, 1¾ cups (350 g) sugar, salt, baking soda, and vanilla extract. Mix in the prepared flaxseed meal. Roll into 1-inch (2.5 cm) balls, place 2 inches (5 cm) apart on 2 ungreased baking sheets, and then sprinkle the tops with the extra sugar. Flatten cookies slightly with a fork to form a crisscross pattern.

Bake for 9 minutes or until slightly golden brown on the edges. Let cool completely before removing from the baking sheets.

NUTRITIONAL ANALYSIS

PER SERVING: 221 CALORIES; 13 G FAT; 7 G PROTEIN; 22 G CARBOHYDRATE; 2 G DIETARY FIBER; 0 MG CHOLESTEROL.

BUTTERSCOTCH AMARETTI

Excellent

The delicate flavors of almond and brown sugar come together to make a slightly chewy and crispy cookie that is *very* hard to resist. Use almond meal made from blanched almonds, such as Bob's Red Mill brand, with no skins in the ground mix, so you achieve a more uniform color and texture throughout.

• • • • • • • • • • • • • • • • • • • YIELD: 36 COOKIES, OR SERVINGS • • • • • • • • • • • • • • • • • • •

3 tablespoons (21 g) flaxseed meal

6 tablespoons (90 ml) water

3 cups (300 g) almond meal

½ teaspoon sea salt

1 cup (200 g) granulated sugar

½ cup (115 g) packed light brown sugar

Preheat the oven to 300°F (150°C, or gas mark 2). Line 2 or 3 baking sheets with parchment paper or silicone mats.

In a medium-size bowl, mix together the flaxseed meal and water and let rest until goopy, about 5 minutes. In a large bowl, stir together the almond meal, sea salt, and both sugars until well combined.

Slowly add the prepared flaxseed meal to the almond meal mixture and beat vigorously until a slightly sticky dough forms. This can be done effortlessly with an electric mixer; otherwise, it takes a bit of elbow grease to bring the dough together. At first your dough will be crumbly, but eventually it will come together into a clumpy dough.

Drop the dough by slightly rounded tablespoonfuls (15 g) onto the prepared baking sheets. You should have 36 cookies. Bake for 30 minutes or until lightly golden brown around the edges.

Let cool on the pan for a few minutes before transferring to wire racks to cool completely before serving.

NUTRITIONAL ANALYSIS

PER SERVING: 78 CALORIES; 4 G FAT; 2 G PROTEIN; 9 G CARBOHYDRATE; 2 G DIETARY FIBER; 0 MG CHOLESTEROL.

SWEETHEART COOKIES

These cookies were the very first recipe I baked all by myself when I was eight years old. I rummaged around in my mother's recipe box and found these little gems and was immediately drawn to them. They were the cookies that sparked my love of baking. Of course, back then they contained eggs, vegetable shortening, butter, and regular all-purpose wheat flour, so I adapted them a tad. And because I love them so much, I call them my "sweetheart cookies."

• • • • • • • • • • • • • • • • • • • YIELD: 30 COOKIES, OR SERVINGS • • • • • • • • • • • • • • • • • • •

1 cup (225 g) nondairy margarine

1 cup (200 g) sugar

2 tablespoons (14 g) flaxseed meal mixed with ¼ cup (60 ml) warm water

1½ teaspoons vanilla extract

1¼ cups (162 g) sorghum flour

¾ cup (118 g) brown rice flour (superfine is best, but not required)

⅔ cup (86 g) potato starch

1 teaspoon xanthan gum

1 teaspoon baking powder

½ teaspoon sea salt

Preheat the oven to 400°F (200°C, or gas mark 6).

In a large bowl or with an electric mixer, cream together the margarine and sugar until smooth. Add the prepared flaxseed meal and vanilla extract and mix together gently.

In a separate bowl, sift together the sorghum flour, brown rice flour, potato starch, xanthan gum, baking powder, and sea salt.

Gradually add the flour mixture to the margarine mixture and stir until all the flour has been added. Mix vigorously (or on medium speed of an electric mixer) until the dough clumps together.

Drop by rounded tablespoonfuls (15 g) onto 2 ungreased cookie sheets about 2 inches (5 cm) apart. You should have 30 cookies. Bake for 8 to 10 minutes or until medium golden brown on the bottoms.

Let cool completely on a wire rack before indulging in one . . . or four.

RECIPE NOTE

For an extra-special presentation, dip one half of each cookie into melted chocolate, and let the coating harden.

NUTRITIONAL ANALYSIS

PER SERVING: 112 CALORIES; 6 G FAT; 1 G PROTEIN; 13 G CARBOHYDRATE; 1 G DIETARY FIBER; 0 MG CHOLESTEROL.

CHOCOLATE HAZELNUT SPREAD

Inspired by Nutella, this vegan version leaves out the cow's milk and focuses on the delicious combination of roasted hazelnuts and rich chocolate with a hint of sweetness bringing it all together. This spread is a perfect topping for crackers or bread, or use it in place of other nut butters, such as peanut butter, in your favorite recipes.

•••••••••••• YIELD: 20 SERVINGS, ABOUT 1 TABLESPOON (15 G) EACH ••••••••••••

2 cups (300 g) whole roasted hazelnuts, skinned

¼ cup (50 g) superfine granulated sugar

¼ cup (20 g) cocoa powder

¼ teaspoon sea salt

¼ cup (60 ml) or more nondairy milk

Combine the hazelnuts, sugar, cocoa powder, and salt in a food processor and blend until crumbly.

Slowly add the nondairy milk, about 1 tablespoon (15 ml) at a time, and blend until smooth. Depending on how dry your roasted hazelnuts are, you may need to add more or less nondairy milk than called for. I find that some of the hazelnuts I use require very little liquid to make a smooth spread, and some require a good bit of nondairy milk to even allow the mixture to blend properly.

Blend in the food processor until very smooth, about 5 minutes. Transfer to a sealed jar and store in the refrigerator up to 2 weeks.

RECIPE NOTES

* To make superfine sugar, simply grind granulated sugar in a clean coffee or spice grinder until very fine.
* If you cannot locate roasted, skinned hazelnuts, it's easy to make your own. Simply preheat your oven to 350°F (180°C, or gas mark 4) and spread the nuts on an ungreased baking sheet. Roast for about 10 minutes or until the skins begin to detach. Let the nuts cool and then transfer to a bowl or colander. Rub briefly with a clean kitchen towel until all skins have been removed.

NUTRITIONAL ANALYSIS

PER SERVING: 60 CALORIES; 5 G FAT; 3 G PROTEIN; 4 G CARBOHYDRATE; 1 G DIETARY FIBER; 0 MG CHOLESTEROL.

CHOCOLATE SALTED CARAMELS

A candy thermometer is extra helpful when making these fun, yet sophisticated, candies. Deep, dark, and slightly salty, these caramels should be savored.

• YIELD: 40 CARAMELS, OR 20 SERVINGS • • • • • • • • • • • • • • • • • •

2 cups (470 ml) canned coconut milk
½ cup (90 g) semisweet chocolate
2 cups (400 g) sugar
1 cup (235 ml) light corn syrup
½ cup (112 g) nondairy margarine
1 tablespoon (15 ml) vanilla extract
Flaky sea salt, for topping

Grease or line with parchment a 9 x 9-inch (23 x 23 cm) baking pan. Or use a silicone baking pan; they work marvelously with caramels and don't need any prep!

In a 2-quart (1.8 L) saucepan, bring the coconut milk to a boil over medium heat and then stir in the chocolate chips until melted. Add the sugar and corn syrup and cook, stirring constantly, until the sugar is completely dissolved.

Add the margarine and stir until the mixture comes to a boil. Once boiling, stop stirring! Let it continue to boil over medium heat, without stirring, until it reaches 240°F (116°C) on your candy thermometer. A good indicator to test for progress, if you are lacking a candy thermometer, is to dip the tip of a wooden spoon into the top of the bubbly mixture. The syrup should stick to the spoon when it is about done. Cooking time is approximately 35 minutes.

If you think it's time, take a teaspoon of the syrup and quickly drop it into a very cold glass of water; if it's ready, you'll be left with what looks like a caramel. This is referred to as the "firm-ball" stage. You will know it is ready when the ball is firm enough to allow you to remove it from the glass with your fingers and will flatten if you give it a little squeeze.

When the mixture is at the right temperature, stir in the vanilla and quickly pour into your prepared pan. Let cool at room temperature for a few minutes and then transfer to the fridge for about 1 hour. Once firm, cut into 40 squares and sprinkle with sea salt. Wrap in waxed paper and store in the fridge.

NUTRITIONAL ANALYSIS

PER SERVING: 138 CALORIES; 8 G FAT; 0 G PROTEIN; 19 G CARBOHYDRATE; 1 G DIETARY FIBER; 0 MG CHOLESTEROL.

ALMOND BUTTER CUPS

This recipe is slightly time-consuming, but that mostly lies in painting the cups with the melted chocolate; after that, it's smooth sailing. If you're a die-hard chocolate and almond fan like I am, these little treats are well worth the effort.

• • • • • • • • • • • • • • • • • • • YIELD: 16 CANDIES, OR SERVINGS • • • • • • • • • • • • • • • • • • •

I bag (12 ounces, or 340 g) nondairy chocolate chips

I cup (250 g) smooth or crunchy unsalted almond butter

I teaspoon vanilla extract

2 tablespoons (15 g) confectioners' sugar

Dash or two of salt

2 tablespoons (30 ml) almond milk

Line about 16 mini muffin cups with mini muffin liners.

In a double boiler over medium-low heat, melt half of the chocolate until smooth.

Drop about 1 teaspoon of melted chocolate into each mini muffin liner and use the back of a spoon to smoosh the chocolate to coat the liners. Aim for making the chocolate about ⅛-inch (3 mm) thick. Chill the chocolate-coated liners in the freezer for about 10 minutes or until solid.

In the meantime, in a small bowl, mix together the almond butter, vanilla extract, confectioners' sugar, salt, and nondairy milk until smooth.

Once the chocolate shells are chilled, fill with the almond butter mixture, dividing evenly among all 16 cups. Chill again in the freezer while you melt the remaining chocolate.

In a double boiler over medium-low heat, melt the remaining half of the chocolate until smooth. Top the filled cups with a smooth layer of chocolate, spreading out to the edges of the paper lining, and chill once again in the freezer until firm, 5 to 10 minutes.

Store the cups in the fridge or freezer in an airtight container and serve chilled.

NUTRITIONAL ANALYSIS

PER SERVING: 197 CALORIES; 14 G FAT; 3 G PROTEIN; 16 G CARBOHYDRATE; 1 G DIETARY FIBER; 0 MG CHOLESTEROL.

MOCK TURTLES

My dad loved "turtle" chocolate candies so much that it was an easy and always appreciated gift for him on any holiday. This is a healthier version of my dad's fave, with a very easy caramel made from Medjool dates.

• • • • • • • • • • • • • • • • • •   YIELD: 20 CANDIES, OR 10 SERVINGS   • • • • • • • • • • • • • • • • • •

20 Medjool dates, pitted

3 tablespoons (45 g) nondairy margarine

1 vanilla bean pod, split lengthwise and seeds scraped

40 whole pecan pieces

4 cups (700 g) nondairy chocolate chips

1 teaspoon coconut oil

In a food processor, combine the Medjool dates, margarine, and scraped vanilla seeds and pulse until uniformly sticky. Scoop out 1 to 2 teaspoons of the mixture, shape into a patty, and place 2 or 3 pecans on top. Flip over so that the pecans are on the bottom. Place on a baking sheet lined with a silicone mat or waxed paper. Repeat with the remaining date mixture and pecans to form 20 candies.

In a double boiler, melt the chocolate over medium-low heat. Stir in the coconut oil.

Dip just the bottoms of the candies into the chocolate to coat evenly and return to the baking sheet. Drizzle the tops with the remaining melted chocolate. Let harden in a cool place for at least 2 hours or until firm. Keep chilled to prevent melting.

NUTRITIONAL ANALYSIS

PER SERVING: 214 CALORIES; 20 G FAT; 3 G PROTEIN; 9 G CARBOHYDRATE; 3 G DIETARY FIBER; 0 MG CHOLESTEROL.

ORANGE JULIA

Modeled after the classic shopping mall treat, this creamy and
dreamy smoothy is a healthier (and more feminine) version of my favorite
childhood drink, the Orange Julius.

YIELD: 4 SERVINGS

1¼ cups (300 ml) frozen orange juice
  (I like to freeze mine in ice cube trays.)

1 cup (235 ml) almond or rice milk

1 banana, peeled, sliced, and frozen

½ teaspoon vanilla bean paste or extract

Extra orange juice or nondairy milk to
  thin, if desired

Blend all the ingredients in a blender until smooth. Serve
immediately and slurp through a straw.

RECIPE NOTE

Instead of drinking, fill up popsicle molds with this recipe after
blending and freeze to make "smoothsicles."

NUTRITIONAL ANALYSIS

PER SERVING: 167 CALORIES; 0 G FAT; 2 G PROTEIN; 40 G CARBOHYDRATE; 2 G DIETARY FIBER; 0 MG CHOLESTEROL.

RASPBERRY LEMONADE

This lemonade, with its sweet and tangy flavor and fun pink color, is sure to please everyone, both young and old.

•••••••••••••••••• YIELD: 10 SERVINGS, 1 CUP (235 ML) EACH ••••••••••••••••••

2 cups (300 g) fresh raspberries

1½ cups (355 ml) lemon juice, divided

2 cups (400 g) sugar

¼ cup (60 ml) plus 8 cups (1.9 L) cold water, divided

In saucepan combine the raspberries, ½ cup (120 ml) of the lemon juice, sugar, and ¼ cup (60 ml) water. Heat over medium heat, stirring constantly and breaking apart the raspberries, until the sugar is dissolved and a chunky syrup is formed. Let cool to room temperature and then mix in the remaining 1 cup (235 ml) lemon juice and the remaining 8 cups (1.9 L) water. Pour into a large pitcher with a strainer attached to the lid or pour through a strainer before transferring to the pitcher. Serve chilled over ice.

NUTRITIONAL ANALYSIS

PER SERVING: 176 CALORIES; 0 G FAT; 0 G PROTEIN; 46 G CARBOHYDRATE; 2 G DIETARY FIBER; 0 MG CHOLESTEROL.

CHOCOLATE PEANUT BUTTER (GREEN) SMOOTHIE

Chocolate and peanut butter make a cunning disguise for the spinach
that hides inside this smoothie, making it the perfect starter "green" smoothie
for both kids and adults!

•   YIELD: 4 SERVINGS   •

1 banana, peeled, sliced, and frozen

1 cup (30 g) packed fresh spinach

2 tablespoons (32 g) creamy
peanut butter

1 teaspoon vanilla extract

1 tablespoon (15 ml) agave nectar

2 to 3 tablespoons (16 to 24 g)
cocoa powder

1 cup (235 ml) very cold water

Place all the ingredients in a blender and blend until smooth.
Divide among 4 glasses and enjoy!

RECIPE NOTE

Any leafy greens can be used in this recipe, but I recommend
spinach for its slightly sweet and neutral flavor. Long-time green
smoothie lovers may enjoy this made with kale, chard, or even
dandelion greens. MMM-mmm.

NUTRITIONAL ANALYSIS

PER SERVING: 95 CALORIES; 5 G FAT; 3 G PROTEIN; 13 G CARBOHYDRATE; 2 G DIETARY FIBER; 0 MG CHOLESTEROL.

CHERRY BERRIES 'N CREAM SMOOTHIE

This sweet smoothie tastes just like cherry ice cream!

1 cup (155 g) chopped fresh cherries
1 cup (145 g) sliced strawberries
1 cup (235 ml) almond milk
½ cup (120 ml) lite canned coconut milk
½ teaspoon almond extract

Place all the ingredients in a blender and blend until smooth. Serve immediately.

Very Cherry Ending

Take this recipe from breakfast to dessert by adding 2 cups (290 g) vanilla bean ice cream (page 37) to your blender along with the other ingredients. Top with whipped cream and crushed toasted almonds.

Nutritional Analysis

Per serving: 130 calories; 9 g fat; 3 g protein; 13 g carbohydrate; 3 g dietary fiber; 0 mg cholesterol.

MOCHACCINO MILKSHAKE

The sultry combo of chocolate and coffee come together perfectly in this thick milkshake. For extra flair, top with whipped coconut cream and nondairy chocolate shavings.

• YIELD: 2 SERVINGS •

3 cups (720 g) nondairy vanilla bean ice cream

¾ to 1 cup (180 to 235 ml) nondairy milk

1 tablespoon (8 g) espresso powder or instant coffee

2 tablespoons (10 g) cocoa powder

Blend all the ingredients in a blender until smooth. Serve immediately.

SWEET IDEA

This milkshake is a perfect beverage to serve with a couple of Sweetheart Cookies (page 192). Add two straws and make it a date.

NUTRITIONAL ANALYSIS

PER SERVING: 169 CALORIES; 4 G FAT; 3 G PROTEIN; 30 G CARBOHYDRATE; 4 G DIETARY FIBER; 0 MG CHOLESTEROL.

WHITE CHOCOLATE AMARETTO HOT COCOA

White chocolate hot cocoa with the subtle flavor of almond makes an intoxicating combo and a perfect beverage for when the temperature dips.

YIELD: 4 SERVINGS

2 cups (470 ml) almond milk

½ cup (75 g) chopped white chocolate chunks (page 38)

¼ cup (50 g) sugar

1 teaspoon almond extract

Dash of salt

Bring the almond milk to a boil over medium heat and then pour over the white chocolate chunks in a heat-safe bowl. Add the sugar, almond extract, and salt and stir until the white chocolate is melted and the sugar is dissolved. Divide among 4 mugs and serve immediately.

RECIPE NOTE

The cocoa butter in the white chocolate has a tendency to separate if left standing. Keep a swizzle stick or straw in the mug to give it a stir if needed.

NUTRITIONAL ANALYSIS

PER SERVING: 216 CALORIES; 9 G FAT; 5 G PROTEIN; 30 G CARBOHYDRATE; 1 G DIETARY FIBER; 0 MG CHOLESTEROL.

VEGAN RESOURCES

◌❧ Books ❧◌

Carol J. Adams. *The Sexual Politics of Meat: A Feminist-Vegetarian Critical Theory.* New York: Continuum Press, 2010.

Brenda Davis and Vesanto Melina. *Becoming Vegan: The Complete Guide to Adopting a Healthy Plant-Based Diet.* Summertown, TN: Book Publishing Company, 2000.

Gary Francione. *Introduction to Animal Rights: Your Child or the Dog?* Philadelphia: Temple University Press, 2000.

Colleen Patrick-Goudreau. *Vegan's Daily Companion: 365 Days of Inspiration for Cooking, Eating, and Living Compassionately.* Beverly, MA: Quarry Books, 2011.

John Robbins. *The Food Revolution: How Your Diet Can Help Save Your Life and Our World.* Newburyport, MA: Conari Press, 2010.

◌❧ Websites ❧◌

VEGAN INFORMATION

Animal Rights: The Abolitionist Approach: www.abolitionistapproach.com

My Face Is on Fire: www.my-face-is-on-fire.blogspot.com

One Green Planet: www.onegreenplanet.org

VeganFM: www.vegan.fm

Vegansaurus: www.vegansaurus.com

Your Daily Vegan: www.yourdailyvegan.com

FASHION, FOOD, AND ACCESSORIES

Cosmo's Vegan Shoppe:
www.cosmosveganshoppe.com

Cruelty Free Face:
www.crueltyfreeface.com

The Discerning Brute:
www.thediscerningbrute.com

Food Fight Vegan Grocery:
www.foodfightgrocery.com

Also, be sure to visit my ever-expanding blogroll at www.manifestvegan.com for a list of some of my favorite vegan blogs.

Movies

Earthlings (2005)

Food, Inc. (2008)

Forks Over Knives (2011)

The Future of Food (2004)

Got the Facts on Milk (2011)

ACKNOWLEDGMENTS

To my husband and best friend, J.D., for supporting me with everything and anything relating to this book and Manifest:Vegan. Also, thank you for simply believing in me.

To my favorite kids in the entire world, Landen and Olive, for inspiring me to do my best in everything I pursue and do it with joy, curiosity, and boundless energy.

To my wonderful literary agency, the Lisa Ekus Group, and notably Sally Ekus, for believing in my ideas, supporting me, and making my cookbookery dreams come true. I couldn't imagine being backed by a better agency and look forward to working with you all for many, many more years to come.

To my awesome editors, Amanda Waddell and Karen Levy, for helping me through my very first book. And special thanks to Betsy Gammons, Kathryn Ahlin, Meg Sniegoski, and everyone else at Fair Winds Press for making this cookbook more incredible than I could have ever imagined.

To my bestie Kelani Edmondson, for helping me kick-start Manifest:Vegan and making it look ten times better than it ever would have without your mad skills and for inspiring me to get some of that CSS knowledge under my own belt. Also, for being a true blue friend after twenty-plus long years. No matter where we both happen to be in the world, you are always right there.

To my sister, Wendi Boggs, for supporting me and my ideas 100 percent. Always.

To my mother, Catherine Cain, for letting me ransack the kitchen during my childhood, for never discouraging me from teaching myself how to cook, and for allowing me to eat anything I wanted. Even when I was too short to open the kitchen cabinets and would make a mess out of everything I touched, I was still allowed to do it all over again the next day. Thank you for that.

To my brother and sister, Larney Cain and Lori Puhala, for sharing and cooking meals with me when I was just a babe.

To Jessy Farrell, for being the other pea in my pod, a damn good friend, and an amazing pen pal during the entirety of this book. Your wisdom and compassion through everything is always very appreciated.

To Kittee Berns and Julie Hasson, for giving me the jump-start to get my ideas "out there" and into book form. Without your help, I would have never had the opportunities I have had with this book. Thank you, truly. You guys rock major striped knee-high socks!

To my incredible testers: Jessica Aichs, Jim Allen, Morgan Mills Blank, Tiffany Cadiz, Monika Soria Caruso, Megan Clarke, Jeffrey Eggleston, Corina and Anthony Goodwin, Katara Jade, Christine Keely, "Tofu" Ted Lai, Heather Lewis, Caitlin McGrother, Jenni Mischel, Lisa Pitman, Jennifer Pitoniak, Melissa Schneider, Kristina@spabettie.com, and Dianne Wenz, CHHC. Without your dedication, thoroughness, and excitement about testing these recipes, this book would have been a *lot* harder to manage. Also, thank you for giving me wonderful ideas for adaptations for a few of the recipes and a much-needed perspective from your own kitchens. You all have provided more help to me than you can even imagine, and I am forever grateful.

To Thomas Macaulay, for teaching me about intention and reworking my ideas until they make sense to someone other than me. This sensibility has become incredibly important in every single thing I do.

To Diane Fitch, for fostering my love of color and composition and for letting me know it is okay to try and make a living out of what I love. Color drives me, and I have you to thank for being able to see it in all its saturated glory.

And last, but absolutely not least, to my readers at manifestvegan.com and fellow food bloggers, every single last one of you: From all of you I have gained inspiration, wisdom, encouragement, friends, and a wonderful group of people with whom to share my recipes. Thank you. Thank you. Thank you.

About the Author

Allyson Kramer is the force behind the popular
vegan and gluten-free recipe blog manifestvegan.com.
She holds a BFA in painting and sculpture and is a
self-taught recipe developer and food photographer.
Allyson has been featured in *VegNews* magazine and on
The Huffington Post and has become an authority on
eating vegan and gluten-free. In her free time she
enjoys hiking, distance running as fast as she can
for as long as she can, bonding with nonhuman animals,
and watching films in any language that's not English.
Raised in a small town outside of Dayton, Ohio,
Allyson currently resides with her husband and
two kids in Philadelphia, Pennsylvania.

INDEX